# THE ULTIMATE
## RECONCILIATION
## AND
## SALVATION OF ALL

GARRY D. PIFER

Interior design: www.fiverr.com freelance services

Cover design: www.fiverr.com freelance services

Proofreader/editor: Anna Hagen

Printed in the United States of America   Published at Edmonton, KY

gdpifer@scrtc.com

*For this is good and acceptable*
*in the sight of God our Saviour,*
*Who will have all men to be saved,*
*and to come unto the knowledge*
*of the truth.*

**1 Timothy 2:3-4**

# DEDICATION

In the Introduction to this book I tell of the visit with friends who shared some of what they were seeing in the Word regarding salvation. It was not only new to my wife and me, but seemed totally against most of what we had been taught all of our lives. But a seed had been planted and as time passed that seed was being watered, fertilized, and cultivated. In this book, what we discovered will be presented to you. We certainly are grateful and thankful for what Mike and Sandra shared with us and I dedicate this book to them.

# CONTENTS

# INTRODUCTION

In the autumn of 1999, while visiting some friends that we had not seen nor heard from for over 25 years, my wife and I were introduced to an aspect of salvation and reconciliation that we had never heard before. We were like most people when presented with something they don't believe or have never heard before, we came up with all kinds of arguments and reasons (in our minds) as to why what we were hearing could not be true. Our friends just asked that we consider and study from our own Bibles what they were sharing. Sadly, we didn't begin that study at that time. However, over the following months and years, we received comments and thoughts from a number of others that added to what we had been introduced to. Finally, after about three years, we felt we had to study this subject, and when we did we received some most wonderful revelation.

What were we introduced to? What were our friends seeing from their own Bibles that we had never seen nor heard? They saw in many Scriptures that ultimately God would reconcile and bring all of mankind to salvation. How could that possibly be true? We had been taught, and believed, that we were all "free moral agents," or as most term it, we had free will. Understanding that we could accept or reject God, we could not see how their view could possibly be correct. Possibly our belief in free will needed to be looked at.

1

Like most believers, we had been taught that there was a lake of fire, where those who didn't accept Jesus were to be cast. Some taught that those cast into this fire would be tormented and would be subject to these flames for eternity. The church I had been a part of for most of my life taught a "kinder" version, teaching that those who were the "incorrigible" would be burned up, dying the "second death." If either of these teachings were correct, then how would it be possible that everyone could be saved? Could one or both of these teachings be wrong? Perhaps fire, as used in the Bible, didn't mean what we thought? It was looking as if we had more areas to study.

There were many other things that kept coming to our minds that seemed to prevent what we were being told from possibly being true. We knew that many people died without ever "making a decision" or perhaps even hearing the name and message of Jesus. Isn't today the day of salvation? Would God save people without them believing on and confessing the name of Jesus? How could our friends' understanding square up with all of these things? Could God even save everyone IF He wanted to?

In the following pages we will look at these questions, and then we will look at the numerous scriptures our friend had been sharing with us. Without the foundation that must be laid by looking at the many questions that were raised, it would be nearly impossible to understand what we were being exposed to. Hopefully, sharing what we found from our study will help you to grasp, along with us, the truth of what God has planned.

# CHAPTER ONE

# WHAT ABOUT FREE WILL?

Checking on the internet I found numerous statements regarding what is commonly referred to as "free will." Here are a few statements (without giving any credits) I found. "God, who has all power and all wisdom, has given each person a free will, which God respects within His Laws." "When God created mankind, He gave him something very unique. Man received a free will, so that he could make his own choices according to his own free will." "God is too much of a gentleman to impose His will on you." "It's a spiritual law: God can't violate your free will."

Let us briefly look at this widely held teaching. Several books could be written (and many have been). We can search high and low and we will never find any mention of "free will" in the Scriptures. The words never appear in the Bible. Where did this come from? The problem of free will has been identified in ancient Greek philosophical literature. This notion of free will has been attributed to both Aristiotle (4th century BCE) and Epictetus (1st century CE). The term "free will" (*liberum arbitrium*) was introduced by Christian philosophy (4th century CE).

Augustine (one of the Latin fathers of the Catholic Church who lived from 354-430 and who was greatly influenced by Plato and Aristotle, among others) held views on free will and predestination that would go on to have a profound impact on Christian theology. It has been noted that the various beliefs of free will and predestination have been debated in great depth among Christians over the years. Martin Luther, of the Great Reformation, appears to have rejected free will. It is interesting to note what the Roman Catholic Church declared at the Council of Trent (between 1545-1563), "the free will of man, moved and excited by God, can by its consent co-operate with God, Who excites and invites its action; and that it can thereby dispose and prepare itself to obtain the grace of justification. The will can resist grace if it chooses. It is not like a lifeless thing, which remains purely passive. Weakened and diminished by Adam's fall, free will is yet not destroyed in the race (Sess. VI, cap. I and v)."

It does not appear that any of these philosophers and early "church fathers" looked to the Word of God, the Bible, to see what it had to say. It also appears that what they arrived at in their beliefs has been accepted by Christianity as a whole. I suggest we need to begin with the Bible. As mentioned earlier, we cannot find a single scripture that mentions free will. There are quite a lot of powerful scriptures that speak of God's will. That is where we will begin.

## GOD'S WILL

Almost all believers view God as being sovereign. The word "sovereign" is not used in the King James Version, however the Greek word *despotes* is used and is translated LORD in a number of places.

One place is Acts 4:24, "LORD, thou art God, which hast made heaven, and earth, and the sea, and all that in them is:" Some translations, such as the English Standard Version and the Weymouth Translation, render this "Sovereign LORD." The Greek *despotes,* Strong's number G1203, is defined by Vines, "a master. Lord. One who possesses supreme authority." God is in absolute authority.

Let us look at what we are told concerning His will. Ephesians 1:11 speaks of God, "In whom also we have obtained an inheritance, being predestinated according to the purpose of him who worketh all things after the council of his own will." Quite a number of translations use almost exactly the same wording and phrases, but several others bring out the meaning perhaps a bit more clearly. Here are several of the other renderings of the last portion of the verse. From the Easy-to-Read Version and the New Century Version, "And he is the one who makes everything agree with what he decides and wants." The New Living Translation translates it this way, "and he makes everything work out according to his plan." The Holman Christian Standard Bible, "the one who works out everything in agreement with the decision of his will." One more, The New Testament in Modern English, J. B. Phillips says "by the one Who achieves his purposes by his sovereign will."

Ephesians 1:11 isn't the only passage that speaks of God's will. Notice a few more. Psalm 135:6, from the English Standard Version, "Whatever the Lord pleases, He does, in heaven and in earth, in the seas and in all deeps." The Passion Translations renders this verse this way, "He does what He pleases, with unlimited power and authority, extending His greatness throughout the entire universe." Isaiah

46:9-10 also speaks powerfully. From the New American Standard Bible of 1995, "For I am God, and there is no other; I am God, and there is no one like Me, declaring the end from the beginning, and from ancient times things which have not been done, saying, 'My purpose will be established, and I will accomplish all My good pleasure.'" Look at what God is saying in Daniel 4:35, again from the New American Standard Bible of 1995, "All the inhabitants of the earth are accounted as nothing, but He does according to His will in the host of heaven and among the inhabitants of earth; and no one can ward off His hand or say to Him, 'What have You done?'" One more verse, from both the English Standard Version and The New American Standard Bible 1995, quoted from Job 42:2, "I know that You can do all things, and that no purpose of Yours can be thwarted."

Reading these verses, without looking at any others, we are told very powerfully that whatever God wills, desires, and plans will come to pass. Even without looking at mankind's will or desire it appears pretty conclusive that it can't thwart what God's will is. Let us look at what the Bible reveals about man's will.

## Mankind's Will

Before we get into the many scriptures that reveal what man's will truly is, I believe we all need to be on the same page as to the definition of "free will." An internet search will yield numerous definitions from philosophy, as well as from Christian and religious sources. Free will has always been a debated topic, it appears. Perhaps the greatest debate was between Desiderius Erasmus and Martin Luther. In 1524 Erasmus wrote a book called *De libero arbitrio,* or *The*

*Freedom of the Will.* In the book Erasmus defines free will as "a power of the human will by which a man can apply himself to the things which lead to eternal salvation or turn away from them." (Martin Luther responded in his own book, On the Bondage of the Will, written in 1525. In the original Latin it was *De Servo Arbitrio,* literally, *'On Un-free Will,'* or *'Concerning Bound Choice.')* The Merriam Webster dictionary defines free will as a noun and gives us two definitions, "1: voluntary choice or decision. 2: freedom of humans to make choices that are not determined by prior causes or by divine intervention."

What does the Word of God, the Bible, tell us about the will of man? Do we have the freedom to choose to be saved or the freedom and ability to reject salvation? Can we, the created, tell God, the Creator, the One who "worketh all things after the counsel of his own will," that we refuse His free gift of salvation "and He can't do anything about it"? Let us look at a few of the many scriptures that reveal mankind's will.

The Apostle Paul had much to say regarding all of mankind, our nature and our will. In Ephesians 2:1 he tells us that we all "were dead in trespasses and sins." Then in verse 3 he continues, telling us that we "were by nature the children of wrath, even as others." Mankind, all of us, Paul says, are in our natural state in rebellion to God. "There is none righteous, no, not one: There is none that understandeth, there is none that seeketh after God." (Romans 3:10-11) None of us seeks salvation, seeks to understand and know God. It is not of our "will" to decide to be saved or to reject salvation. The gospel of Jesus Christ is foolish to man. (1 Cor. 1:18, 2:14) Let us quote the whole verse of 1 Cor. 2:14, "But the natural man receiveth not the things of the Spirit of God: for they are foolishness unto him; neither can he know them, because they are spiritually discerned." Paul penned some very powerful words to the church at Rome. Romans 8:6-7, "For to be carnally minded is death; but to be spiritually minded is life and peace. Because the carnal mind is enmity against God: for it is not subject to the law of God, neither indeed can be." Are we grasping what Paul is revealing to us? In our natural state, with our fleshly mind and of our own will or desire, we are totally incapable of "making a decision for Christ."

Let us notice a few more scriptures written by the Apostle Paul. We were all servants of sin. In Romans 6:20 he tells us that "when ye were the servants of sin, ye were free from righteousness." We were all enslaved to sin. In his letter to the Colossians he tells us that we were hostile toward God, "And you, that were sometime alienated and enemies in your mind by wicked works." Yes, all of us, all of mankind, in our natural, carnal, fleshly state had no will or desire for God or the things of God. God gave us the ability to make choices, and even told us what to choose, but that never enabled us to decide to get saved or to reject salvation.

## GOD'S WILL VS. MANKIND'S WILL

Jesus told us that "No man can come to me, except the Father which sent me draw him:" (John 6:44) He says "No man." That means none, no one, not any. The definition of the word "draw," Strong's number G1670, *helkuo, helko,* is "to drag (literally of figuratively), draw." Vine's indicates that it is used "of a more vigorous action." Coming to Jesus isn't something one just decides by his own "free will" to do. A few verses earlier (John 6:37) Jesus said "All that the Father giveth me shall come to me;" In other words, all of us must be made willing.

The apostle Paul tells us numerous times that we DID NOT choose God or Jesus. We were chosen by God. Ephesians 1:4 says, "According as he **hath chosen us** in him before the foundation of the world." In his first letter to the church at Corinth Paul states very clearly that it is God who chose us. Let us look at what he says, 1 Cor. 1:26-30, "For ye see your calling, brethren, how that not many wise men after the flesh, not many mighty, not many noble are called: But God hath **chosen** the foolish things of the world to confound the wise; and God hath **chosen** the weak things of the world to confound the things which are mighty; And the base things of the world, and things which are despised, hath God **chosen**, yea, and things which are not, to bring to nought things that are: That no flesh should glory in his presence. But of him (and it is all God's doing-Weymouth Translation) are ye in Christ Jesus, who of God is made unto us wisdom, and righteousness, and sanctification, and redemption." To cap this off Paul adds in the next verse, verse 31, "That according as it is written, LET HIM THAT GLORIETH, LET HIM GLORY IN THE LORD." Paul makes it plain in verse 30 that believers (in Corinth or today) were "in Christ Jesus" (were believers) not because of Paul's doing or by their own "free will," but by Him who chose. It was God's doing. It was God's will, not a result of each man's own "free will," but by Him who chose. It was God's doing. It was God's will, not a result of each man's own "fee will." (Emphasis mine.)

Paul taught the same thing to the church at Rome. He tells them, and us, "So then it is not of him that willeth, nor of him that runneth, but of God that sheweth mercy." (Rom. 9:16) In the context of Romans 9, Paul is talking about how men receive God's mercy. That mercy doesn't depend upon a man's will, nor does it depend on how a man may "run," which is referring to his works, how he is living. Rather, it depends entirely on God, the one who extends mercy according to His will.

Paul tells us a bit more about God and the salvation that we receive from Him. "For by grace are ye saved through faith; and that not of yourselves: it is the gift of God." (Eph. 2:8) He continues with the next couple of verses, "Not of works (nothing that we did through "free will"), lest any man should boast." (vs. 9) Verse 10 tells us once again that we didn't have anything to do with it by any "will" of our own. "For we are his workmanship, created in Christ Jesus unto good works, which God hath before ordained that we should walk in them."

In his letter to the Galatians Paul tells us again that it is by "the faith of Jesus Christ" that we received justification. "Knowing that a man is not justified by the works of the law, but **by the faith of Jesus Christ**, even we have believed in Jesus Christ, that we might be justified **by the faith of Christ**,

and not by the works of the law: for by the works of the law shall no flesh be justified." (Gal. 2:16, emphasis mine) Although Paul stated two times in this verse that it was **by the faith of Jesus Christ** that we were justified, he repeats it again in verse 20. "I am crucified with Christ: nevertheless I live; yet not I, but Christ liveth in me: and the life I now live in the flesh I live **by the faith of the Son of God**, who loved me, and gave himself for me." (emphasis mine)

Repentance is an absolute necessity for receiving salvation. We do not, nor can we, come to repentance by our own "free will." We are told over and over again that repentance is something we are granted, something that we are given. Let us look at a few scriptures. Rom. 2:4, "Or despiseth thou the riches of his goodness and forbearance and longsuffering; not knowing that the goodness of God **leadeth thee to repentance?**" Acts 5:31, "Him hath God exalted with his right hand to be a prince and a Saviour, for to **give repentance** to Israel, and forgiveness of sins." Acts 11:18, "When they heard these things, they held their peace, and glorified God, saying, Then hath God also to the Gentiles **granted repentance** unto life." 2 Tim. 2:25, "In meekness instructing those that oppose themselves; if God peradventure will **give them repentance** to the acknowledging of the truth." (emphasis mine)

Checking the definition of repentance in an English language dictionary, we are most often told that it is along the line of "feeling remorse or regret." Most Christian sources will tell us that it means "to change the mind." I believe that it is more than just feeling a need to make a 180 degree turn in what one believes. True repentance has to do with the will, our carnal nature. In appendix 111 of Bullinger's Companion Bible we find the definition that comes very close to that. The Greek word, a noun, translated "repentance," is *metanoia,*

G3341. Let me quote from Dr. Bullinger: "...*metanoia* = a real change of mind and attitude toward sin itself, and the **cause** of it (not merely the **consequence** of it." Then he continues with the definition I'd like us to take special note of. "It has been defined as a change in our principle of action from what is by nature the exact opposite." He is speaking of the very nature of man that we looked at earlier, our natural "will." The change to that nature, our "will," comes only by God's work of giving, granting, and leading us to that true repentance. He exercises His will toward us, dealing with our nature, doing what is impossible in the natural.

There is much more to be understood about "free will." Before we continue on through this book, let us look at a couple of Biblical examples of God bringing individuals to a change, a reversal of the natural will. We'll see that He doesn't force a change but leads one to make the change, a change they could or would never do by their own "free will."

## THE PROPHET JONAH

We won't spend a lot of time but most of us are familiar with the story of Jonah. From all indications, Jonah was a prophet with a relationship of some sort with God. In the first verse of chapter 1 of the book of Jonah we find that God spoke to Jonah. In verse 2 we are told what God told him to do. In verse 3 we find Jonah's "free will." He decided, according to his own "free will," that he didn't want to go and preach the warning to Nineveh. He attempted to flee from God. As we see in the story, that doesn't work. God's will is much greater.

As we continue to read the story we find what God does. We do not find that God forced Jonah to do what He had instructed him to do. First we are told that God "sent out a great wind into the sea." (verse 4) After a bit of discussion among those on the ship, it was revealed that Jonah was the one responsible for the storm and the eminent destruction of the ship. Jonah told them he was fleeing from God and that they needed to throw him overboard. They hesitated to do this but, as they were not making any headway, they finally took Jonah and tossed him into the sea.

But that wasn't the end of God's actions. He "prepared a great fish to swallow up Jonah." (verse 17 of chapter 1) Jonah's attitude and will began to change. He prayed to God, and God heard him. However, God let Jonah search his innermost thoughts and his will for 3 days and 3 nights before God spoke to the fish and instructed it to vomit Jonah out onto the shore. God didn't force Jonah, but He made things uncomfortable, encouraging Jonah to come to a change in his thinking, his attitude, and his will.

## SAUL ON THE ROAD TO DAMASCUS

In Acts 7:58 we read of a man named Saul who was there when Stephen was stoned. He was right in the front of the crowd, with those doing the stoning placing their clothing at his feet. Chapter 8 verse 1 tells us that Saul was not just a spectator but was "consenting unto his death." Verse 3 says he "made havock of the church" and was committing both men and women to prison. When we come to chapter 9 verse 1 we find that apparently some time had passed, but

Saul was "yet breathing out threatenings and slaughter against the disciples" of Jesus.

He obtained letters of authorization to the synagogues in Damascus that he might apprehend and bring to Jerusalem any that he found of "this way." In verses 3-6 we read of the event that occurred on the road as he traveled to Damascus. There was a bright light that shined about him and, as we read on, we find that he was blinded. He was struck down to the ground, and he heard the voice of Jesus asking him why he was persecuting Him. Saul recognized that there was authority behind that voice and addressed Jesus as LORD. He was trembling and was "astonished." He inquired as to what he was to do. Jesus could have given him his "assignment" then and there, but He told him to go into the city and he would be told. Saul had 3 days of blindness (verse 9) in which I'm sure God's Spirit was working to bring about greater changes in his attitude and will, and bring him to repentance. Again, neither God nor Jesus forced Saul, but Saul was changed by the power of the Holy Spirit. In verse 15 we read that the LORD had plans for Saul. He had chosen him for a very special job and God's WILL prevailed over what Saul had been attempting to do, by exercising his own will.

# CHAPTER TWO

# IS THIS THE ONLY DAY OF SALVATION?

It seems that practically every Christian church in the world believes that today, right now in this age, is the only day of salvation. Is this true? Is this a belief that is based on Scripture, or on tradition that has been passed down for centuries? Consider this. IF this teaching and belief is correct there is no hope for the millions and billions of people who have lived and died never having heard the name of Jesus, who we view as the lost and unsaved dead. However, we are going to look at many of the dozens of scriptures from the Bible that don't support this teaching. We will see that the Bible reveals that these individuals, perhaps some of your loved ones, do have a future and are not lost forever.

Almost all proponents of this teaching quote 2 Corinthians 6:2. It states, "For he saith, I have heard thee in a time accepted, and in the day of salvation have I succoured thee: behold, now is the accepted time; behold, now is the day of salvation." At first glance and at first reading it certainly does seem that now is the ONLY time one can be saved. Sadly, if this be true, 98% of all of mankind that has lived since the time of Adam are lost with no hope of ever receiving salvation. And that includes many, if not most, of our friends and family. Let us look a bit deeper than the first surface reading of this verse.

From all we are able to understand, the apostle Paul wrote this letter to the church at Corinth in the Greek language. Most of us, having learned and used the English language all of our lives, may find it a bit difficult to grasp, but the Greek language (and also Hebrew) has no definite or indefinite articles. That means that there are no equivalents to such words as "the" or "a." In the verse we are considering, the Greek would have been "now is day of salvation." The word "the" was supplied by the translators. Is this what Paul had in mind? Young's Literal Bible, which overall is one of the most faithful to the original language (although not always with the most clarity) renders this verse this way: "for He saith, 'In an acceptable time I did hear thee, and in a day of salvation I did help thee, lo, now is a well-accepted time; lo, now, a day of salvation,' -" This verse is quoted from Isaiah 49:8 and is also translated in Young's Literal Bible as "a day of salvation."

## RESURRECTION

One of the foundational doctrines outlined in Hebrews chapter six is "resurrection of the dead." Most have some idea of what the resurrection of the dead is, but most don't truly know all that is taught us from Scripture. When we study the subject, we find revelation regarding the/a "day of salvation." We won't be able to go into all that the Bible has for us in this short chapter, but we will try to draw our attention to the words regarding salvation.

Let us begin in 1 Corinthians chapter 15, often referred to as the "resurrection chapter." Paul begins his teaching in verse 12 where he says that some of those he is addressing there in Corinth are saying there is no resurrection of the dead. He tells us that if there is no resurrection, then Jesus has not been raised, and we are still in our sins. Let us notice verse 20, "But now is Christ risen from the dead, and become the firstfruits of them that slept (have died)." In verse 22 he relates that in Adam ALL die. There is no escaping death. He continues and tells us that in Christ "shall ALL be made alive. This is the same ALL.

In verse 23 is a very interesting statement. Continuing his statement that ALL would be resurrected, he states that they will be raised "every man in his own order." The Greek word translated "order" is *tagma*, Strong's number G5001. It means in an orderly arrangement and **"a series or succession."** (emphasis mine) It is interesting to note that this is the only place in the Bible where this word is used. Paul gives us a bit of information as to that order. Continuing in verse 23, "Christ the firstfruits; afterward they that are Christ's at his coming." In 1 Thessalonians 4:16 these are referred to as "the dead in Christ," indicating those drawn to Jesus by the Father, given the faith of Jesus and repentance, and who had died the physical death Paul stated that we all die. In other words, those who were born again, those given salvation in this age. In verse 17 he tells us that those born again believers who are still alive will be caught up with those resurrected.

Coming back to chapter 15 of 1 Corinthians, Paul states in verse 24, "then cometh the end." It seems apparent, especially when we look at other passages speaking of resurrection that there is a period of time that passes before "the end" he is speaking of comes to pass. We will look at some of those passages in a moment, but let us consider something else that Paul has told us here. He says in verse 20 and verse 23 that Christ is the "firstfruits" of those that slept, the dead in Christ. He is truly the "first of the firstfruits." WE, the saved of this age, are called firstfruits.

Let us notice a couple of scriptures. First, James 1:18, "Of his own will begat he us with the word of truth, that we should be a kind of firstfruits of his creatures." What does "firstfruits" convey? Yes, there are additional fruits to come. 2 Thessalonians 2:13 says in the King James Version "God hath from the beginning chosen you to salvation." The English Standard Version and a few others makes this a bit clearer. The English Standard says, "God chose you as the firstfruits to be saved." The International Version is much the same, "God chose you to be the first fruits for salvation." The Amplified Bible, Classic Edition, renders it this way, "God chose you from the beginning as His firstfruits (first converts) for salvation." What we are being told is that those of us brought to salvation during this age are just the first, the small harvest, of all to be saved.

We won't take the time here to expound in depth that Jesus was the Wave Sheaf Offering. (For a much more detailed study please see chapter thirteen of my book **Shadows of Jesus in the Exodus.**) If you have studied the festivals of God given to the Israelites, you will probably recall that they were to wave a sheaf, or an omer, of the barley before any harvesting of the crop was to commence, before the "sickle was put to the grain." That barley harvest lasted seven weeks (or 50 days) until what we now call Pentecost. At that point a new harvest began, the wheat harvest. Later in the Fall was the feast of ingathering, the larger harvest of grapes, olives, and other crops. Without a lot of explanation here, those saved following the lifting up of Jesus as our Wave Sheaf Offering are those of us in this age. The wheat harvest will be those brought to Jesus during the 1000 year reign. The great harvest will be after the 1000 years.

## THE MILLENNIUM

We will look at Revelation chapter 20. We won't read every word; you can do that on your own.

In verses 1 and 2 we read of the adversary being bound. John states in verse 4 that he saw thrones and judgment given. He mentions those that had been killed and those that remained faithful during their persecution. He says all of these "lived and reigned with Christ a thousand years." A bit more on the "reigning" in a moment, but we are told of more to be resurrected. Verse 5, "But the rest of the dead lived not again until the thousand years were finished." He gives a statement referring back to what had been given in the previous verses, "This is the first resurrection." Verse 6 tells us that those of us in that first resurrection, the one that occurred at Jesus' return, are blessed and holy. Please notice with me what else we are told. We, those of us in the first resurrection, "shall reign with him a thousand years."

You have probably known and even quoted Revelation 1:6 where we are told that Jesus "hath made us kings and priests." To be a king we must have others we are reigning over. IF everyone that is given salvation were made a king, who would there be to rule over? That would mean that everyone is in charge. You and I both know that wouldn't work. John also states here in Revelation 20:6 that those in the first resurrection "shall be priests of God and of Christ." What is the job of a priest? Look with me at Malachi 2:7, "For the priest's lips should keep knowledge, and they should seek the law at his mouth: for he is the messenger of the LORD of hosts." IF we are to be kings and priests – and we see that is the job of those saved in this age and in the first resurrection – we must have people who need to be taught the Word of God. Those people will be the people living this physical life, and their offspring, when Jesus returns and begins His 1000-year rule of the nations, often referred to as "the Millennium." This will be another day of salvation.

## A Great White Throne

We were told in verse 5 of Revelation 20 that "the rest of the dead lived not again until the thousand years were finished." Coming now to verses 11 and 12 we are shown a great white throne and "the dead, small and great" were resurrected and stood before the throne. There has been much taught by various individuals concerning this time. Most are of the opinion that all of the billions of "unsaved" will rise up to stand before God, and the pronouncement will be made that they are to be cast into an ever burning hell fire to be tormented for all of eternity. This is a diabolical teaching of the devil himself. According to what we read in 1 Corinthians 15 these individuals will be raised "every man in his own order," not in one gigantic resurrection of billions at one time. And, what happens when they are raised? Verses 12 and 13 tell us. They are to be judged "according to their works." What works and when? Most assume it was whatever they did or didn't do during their lives, before their death and this resurrection. Part of the lack of understanding is that most don't grasp what judgment is.

Those of us that will be in that first resurrection, the better resurrection referred to in Hebrews 11:35, are being judged now, in this present life and age. Notice 1 Peter 4:17, "For the time is come that judgment must begin at the house of God:" Judgment is so often thought to be a declaration and pronouncement of a sentence. However, in this context, judgment is a process by which we are being brought to a fuller maturity in Christ, being cleaned up and purified, being prepared to be the kings and priests to reign with Christ. This is a study that we each need to do. It isn't within the scope of this book to go into great depth here. But, we might want to consider the last part of Isaiah 26:9, "for when thy judgments are in the earth, the inhabitants of the world will learn righteousness."

What we are being told here in Revelation 20 concerning the great white throne is that, as the "small and great" dead are resurrected to a physical life, they are drawn to Jesus Christ. They will be given faith and repentance, their "will" and very nature will be given a change. They will then be "judged" according to their works. This is "the day of salvation" for each one of them.

# Today is NOT the Only Day of Salvation

Reviewing what we have looked at, we see that the "firstfruits," are being given their "day of salvation" in this life. Those physical people living on into the 1000 years of Jesus' reign, and their offspring, will be drawn to Jesus, given the faith and repentance for salvation, have their "will" acted upon, and be taught and ministered to by those kings and priests that were in the first resurrection. After the 1000 years the rest of the dead, the small and the great who have lived and died since the time of Adam, will be resurrected in "his own order." This will be their "day of salvation."

# CHAPTER THREE

# WHAT ABOUT THE LAKE OF FIRE?

One of the primary doctrines of Christianity is of an ever burning hell where unbelievers will spend eternity being tortured in flames. It is a diabolical doctrine that does not come from the Bible. I know that is a strong statement, but have you ever asked yourself some of the following questions?

If hell is real, why didn't God warn mankind right at creation? God told Adam and Eve the penalty for eating of the tree of the knowledge of good and evil was death, not eternity in fire and brimstone.

If hell is real, why didn't God warn Cain about it, or Sodom and Gomorrah, or any of the others who committed sins early on?

If hell is real, why didn't Moses warn the Israelites about this fate somewhere in the Ten Commandments or in the Law of Moses?

Although the King James Version of the Bible translates the Hebrew word *sheol,* which means the grave or a pit, 31 times as "hell," most other translations DO NOT have the English word HELL in the entire Old Testament. Here are a few that DO NOT have HELL at all: American Standard Version, New American Standard Version, Revised Standard Version, New Revised Standard Version, Revised English Bible, New Living Translation, Amplified Version, New International Version, Darby Translation, New Century Version, Young's Literal Translation, Rotherham's Emphasized Bible, Jewish Publication Society Bible, Tanakh (The Holy Scriptures, Old Testament), plus many, many others.

If hell is real, why did the Apostle Paul, who wrote nearly two-thirds of the New Testament, NEVER warn people of it? If hell is real, wouldn't Paul, of all people, warn us of it repeatedly? Yet, never once does he do so!

A complete book would need to be written to do a complete in-depth teaching on the subject of hell. That is not within the scope of this book. What we will do here is look at what the Bible says, and doesn't say, about the "lake of fire."

## VERSES THAT MENTION THE LAKE OF FIRE

There are only five verses that mention the lake of fire, and they are all found in the book of Revelation. Let us look at all five and then look at what we are being told.

Rev. 19:20 "And the beast was taken, and with him the false prophet that wrought miracles before him, with which he deceived them that had received the mark of the beast, and them that worshipped his image. These both were cast alive into a lake of fire burning with brimstone."

Rev. 20:10 "And the devil that deceived them was cast into the lake of fire and brimstone, where the beast and false prophet are, and shall be tormented day and night for ever and ever."

Rev. 20:14 "And death and hell were cast into the lake of fire. This is the second death."

Rev. 20:15 "And whosoever was not written in the book of life was cast into the lake of fire."

Rev. 21:8 "But the fearful, and unbelieving, and the abominable, and murderers, and whoremongers, and sorcerers, and idolaters, and all liars, shall have their part in the lake which burneth with fire and brimstone: which is the second death."

One thing these verses have in common is that they are all from the book of Revelation. In listening to the numerous individuals who quote and teach from this book, one thing that becomes apparent is that many take some passages as literal and other passages as being symbolic. It seems that the individual chooses which way to view them from their own personal view. But, one needs only to look to the first verse of the first chapter of the book to determine how to look at what we are given. Revelation 1:1, "The Revelation of Jesus Christ, which God gave unto him, to shew unto his servants things which must shortly come to pass; and he sent and signified it by his angel unto his servant John." Did you catch that? I emphasized the word "signified" by putting it in bold characters. What does the word mean? Look at the following.

Strong's definition says "to indicate." Vine's Dictionary of Biblical Words states under the definition for the Greek word *semaino,* Strong's number G4591, "Where perhaps the suggestion is that of expressing by signs." I especially like what Albert Barnes tells us in his commentary of this verse. "He indicated it by signs and symbols." He then continues, "It properly refers to some sign, signal, or token by which anything is made known, and is a word most happily chosen to denote the manner in which the events referred to were to be communicated to John, for nearly the whole book is made up of signs and symbols." We need to be very careful in attaching a literal meaning to verses that are using a symbol.

## FIRE IN THE BIBLE

Few of us associate the word "fire" with the Creator Himself. We generally think of destruction such as Sodom and Gomorrah, or even of the verses we are concentrating on here. However, the attributes of "light" and "heat" from fire speak more of the Creator and His goodness than of a destructive force against His enemies. The writers of the Bible employed the use of "fire" in many different ways. A study of these many ways can be extremely fascinating. We will refer to only a few here. One of the first examples we find is in the covenant God made with Abraham in Genesis 15:17. The King James Version has "a smoking furnace," and a "burning lamp." Other translations have it as "a flaming torch" and "a blazing torch." God appeared to Moses in a burning bush. During the exodus from Egypt,

God was in the pillar of fire. When the covenant was made with Israel at Mt. Sinai God came down in fire and smoke. In Psalms 104:4 it states that God's ministers are "a flaming fire." Even God's Holy Spirit is likened to fire. When it was first given on Pentecost we are told that it "appeared unto them cloven tongues like as of fire." (Acts 2:3)

We most often think of fire as destroying things. We may say things like, "His home was destroyed by fire." We understand what is meant, but actually what has occurred is the components of the house have been changed. The various elements in the wood, for example, have changed forms. Let me try to make this simple. I burn firewood in my stove to heat our home. Combustion is the process by which the elements within the piece of firewood change form. When wood is burned, the heat causes the chemicals from which the wood is composed to vaporize, mixing with the oxygen in the air to form new chemicals, including water and the gas carbon dioxide. What was formerly a tree is no longer in the form of a tree, but the substance thereof is simply CHANGED into a DIFFERENT FORM and exists in its new form. The change is not a physical change but a chemical change. Thus, to burn means to CHANGE.

Fire changes things. A major change a fire makes is that it PURIFIES. Most of us don't realize that many of our English words speak of this. The Greek word translated "fire" in the New Testament is *pur* (pronounced poor), Strong's Number G4442. This Greek word is the root of many of our English words: PURe, PURity, PURify, PURge, PURification. The basic thread is that of purifying. The Hebrew word for fire has much the same meaning. A prophetic passage we should look at is found in the book of Malachi, chapter 3: 1-3.

"Behold, I will send my messenger, and he shall prepare the way for me: and the LORD, whom ye seek, shall suddenly come to his temple, even the messenger of the covenant, whom ye delight in: behold, he shall come, saith the LORD of hosts. But who may abide the day of his coming? And who shall stand when he appeareth? For he is like a refiner's fire, and like fullers' soap: And he shall sit as a refiner and purifier of silver: and he shall purify the sons of Levi, and purge them as gold and silver, that they may offer unto the LORD an offering in righteousness."

## THE FIRE OF GOD

It should be clear to us that the "fire" being depicted is likened to literal fire but is of a spiritual nature. Remember we are looking at a sign or symbol. We just looked at the passage in Malachi which speaks of purifying and purging the sons of Levi. This is the "fire of God." Let us notice a few things that substantiate this. In Luke 3:16 John the Baptist speaking of Jesus says, "He shall baptize you with the Holy Ghost and with fire." The word translated "and" is the Greek word *kai*, Strong's number G2532. It is most often translated "and," however other accurate translations are "also, even, indeed, but." It is translated "even" over 500 times in the New Testament. What John was stating is that the Holy Ghost, or Holy Spirit, is a spiritual fire.

Looking at the five verses which speak of the "lake of fire" we find three of them also include "brimstone." The Greek word is

28

*theion*, Strong's number G2303. Strong's definition is "sulphur." Thayer's adds "divine incense." Vine's says "originally denoted 'fire from heaven.'" Charles Pridgeon (president and founder of the Pittsburgh Bible Institute, 1863-1932) comments about "brimstone" and refers to the Liddell and Scott Greek-English Lexicon, 1897 Edition.[1] He says, "The word *theion* translated 'brimstone' is exactly the same word *theion* which means 'divine.' Sulfur was sacred to the deity among the ancient Greeks; and was used to fumigate, to purify, and to cleanse and to consecrate to the deity;" He continues a bit further on, "The verb derived from *theion* is *theioo*, which means to hallow, to make divine, or to dedicate to a god." It is here that he refers to Liddell and Scott. Mr. Pridgeon then comments, "To any Greek, or to any trained in the Greek language, a 'lake of fire and brimstone' would mean a 'lake of divine purification.'"

The apostle Paul also speaks of this fire, the fire of God. We won't quote the entire passage but just a couple of verses from 1 Corinthians chapter 3. Speaking about our foundation being Jesus Christ, he speaks of men building with gold, silver, precious stones, wood, hay, and stubble. Let us pick up his words in verses 13-15. "Every man's work shall be made manifest: for the day shall declare it, because it shall be revealed by fire; and the fire shall try every man's work of what sort it is. If any man's work abide which he hath built thereupon, he shall receive a reward. If any man's work shall be burned, he shall suffer loss; but he himself shall be saved; yet so as by fire."

---

1 Charles Pridgeon, Is Hell Eternal? Or Will God᾽s Plan Fail? Chapter Eleven

Can we understand what John is telling us in these five verses about "the lake of fire and brimstone"? Those individuals "cast" into the "lake" will have the purifying divine fire of God working upon them to burn up the works built with "wood, hay, and stubble." The "lake of fire" is not to burn up, nor destroy, nor torment these individuals for all eternity. "But wait" some of you may be saying. "Revelation 20:10 says, that they 'shall be tormented day and night for ever and ever'?" Yes, that is what the King James Version says. Once again the translation is the issue. The Greek word translated "ever" (2 times) is *aion*, Strong's number G165. Strong's definition is "properly an age." Vine's also says "an age." Among a number that translate this passage as "ages of the ages" are Literal Translation of the Bible, Weymouth New Testament, and Young's Literal Translation. The time that this purifying takes may be quite some length of time, but it ends when the purifying has been accomplished by the action of the Divine Fire of God.

Earlier we looked at verse 12 of Revelation 20 where we are told of the dead, small and great, and the judgment that was to be upon them. As we continue reading we are told that "death and hell" delivered up the dead. We won't spend the time here to substantiate it but "hell" simply means the grave. Verse 14 has a statement that has been the basis of much doctrinal debate, "This is the second death." This phrase answers the first part of the verse, "And death and hell were cast into the lake of fire." When the work of the Divine Fire is done there will no longer be any death or any graves. Their ending is "the death of death." We were told in 1 Corinthians 15, the resurrection chapter, verse 26, "The last enemy that shall be destroyed is death."

# CHAPTER FOUR

# WHAT ABOUT PREDESTINATION?

Predestination is a widely held belief among Christians. Even so there appears to be no consensus as to just what that belief is. Here are a few definitions and explanations that one can find when doing a brief search on the internet. These are random without referencing sources.

"Since the first century, the church has engaged in debates regarding the finer points of theology. Predestination is one such topic, a source of controversy for centuries."

"Most modern denominations hold to one of two interpretations: the prescient view or the Reformed view. The prescient view is often associated with a school of theology called Arminianism. Simply put this view holds that God chooses who will be saved based upon whether or not a person will respond to the gospel in faith. The Reformed view is often connected along with a larger group of doctrines known as Calvinism. The Reformed view understands predestination to refer to God's unconditional, sovereign choice to save some people and not others."

"Predestination in Christianity is the doctrine that God has eternally chosen whom He intends to save, and is subject to the free decision of the human moral will."

"The notion of double predestination, commonly identified with Calvinism and appearing in some of the writings of St. Augustine and Martin Luther, states that God has determined from eternity whom He will save and whom He will damn, regardless of their faith, love, or merit or lack thereof."

"Predestination is the biblical doctrine that God in His sovereignty chooses certain individuals to be saved."

From these few quotations (among many similar ones I looked at) I have a few initial observations before we look further. It appears the varied beliefs come from various people regarded as scholars, theologians, or "church fathers." It appears that all hold to the false teaching of "free will." (If you need to do so, please review Chapter One.) Although not stated in so many words it comes across to me that the belief that today is the only day of salvation is assumed. (See Chapter Two.)

## WHAT THE BIBLE SAYS ABOUT PREDESTINATION

The Greek word translated "predestinate," "predestinated," and in some verses "before," "determined," and "ordained" is *proorizo*, Strong's number G4309. It is a compound word from the Greek word *pro*, number G4253, and *horizo*, number G3724. *Pro* is defined "fore, in front of, prior." The definition of *horizo* is "declare, determine, limit." *Proorizo* is defined "to predetermine, decide beforehand, determine before." The Greek word is used only six times in the Bible. We'll look at all six.

All but one are found in the writings of the apostle Paul. Let us look first at the one place *proorizo* is used other than in Paul's writings, Acts 4:28, "For to do whatsoever thy hand and thy counsel determined before to be done." The phrase "determined before" is from *proorizo*. Let us look at the context here to see what is being said. Going back to the beginning of chapter three, we read of the miraculous healing of the forty year old man who was lame from birth. We find that, when we come to chapter four, the religious leaders are quite upset about this, and Peter and John are apprehended and put "in hold" overnight. Peter, filled with the Holy Spirit, gave a very powerful message the next day. There was quite a crowd there (verse 4 says about five thousand when they were taken, possibly more when they were brought to "trial.") Afterwards the leaders, not finding how they might punish them, threatened them and let them go.

Then we come to the verses that show exactly what was going on when verse 28 was given. We are told, verse 23, they (Peter and John) returned to their own "company," or the fellow believers. Verse 24 tells us that, upon hearing all that had taken place, they joined together "with one accord" and offered up praise to God. The last half of verse 24 through verse 30 is their prayer recorded for us. In verse 27 they speak of Jesus, God's "holy child," whom God the Father had anointed. They recounted what the government leaders, Herod and

Pilate, along with the Gentiles and the people of Israel gathered to do. Again notice what verse 28 states, "for to do whatsoever thy (God's) hand and thy (God's) counsel **determined before** (predestinated) to be done."

Other scriptures tell us exactly what God had **determined before**. In Peter's inspired message on the day of Pentecost, speaking of Jesus, he says, Acts 2:23, "Him, being delivered by the determinate counsel and foreknowledge of God, ye have taken, and by wicked hands have crucified and slain." One of the two Greek words that make up the word *proorizo*, which is translated predestinated in English, is *horizo*. This is the Greek word used here and translated "determinate." The word "foreknowledge" is translated from the Greek word *prognosis*, Strong's number G4268, and simply means to "know before."

Another verse with similar wording and giving us the same revelation is 1 Peter 1:20. Speaking of Jesus Christ, the Lamb without blemish or spot that was sacrificed for each of us, Peter says, "Who verily was foreordained before the foundation of the world, but was manifest in these last times for you." "Foreordained" is from the Greek word *proginosko*, Strong's number G4267. It means "to know beforehand." It was known, planned, and determined before man was made by God and placed on this earth, that Jesus would come and die on the cross to provide salvation for all of us. You will remember that He came to be "the Savior of the world." Not some of the world, not just a few, but all. We'll speak of this in more detail later in the book.

A couple more verses came to mind when we read Acts 2:23. We read that Jesus was delivered by the "determinate counsel" of God. Go with me to Isaiah verses 10 and 11. "Declaring the end from the beginning, and from ancient times the things that are not yet done, saying, My counsel shall stand, and I will do all my good pleasure; calling a ravenous bird from the east, the man that executeth my counsel from a far country: yea, I have spoken it, I will also bring it to pass; I have purposed it, I will also do it."

## THE INSPIRED WORDS OF THE APOSTLE PAUL

As we mentioned earlier, the other verses where the Greek word *proorizo* is used were all penned by the apostle Paul. Let us examine them. The consensus is that 1 Corinthians was written just prior to the book of Romans and the letter to the church at Ephesus a few years later. The verses we wish to look at are in these three books, so let us read them in the order they were most likely written.

## 1 CORINTHIANS 2:7

1 Corinthians 2:7, "But we speak the wisdom of God in a mystery, even the hidden wisdom, which God ordained before the world unto our glory." The word "ordained" is translated from *proorizo*. In chapter 1 Paul tells the believers in Corinth that in this age God has not called and chosen many of the wise, mighty, and noble according to the flesh. He tells them, and us, that God has chosen the "foolish" of the world, which confounds the wise. As we saw earlier in this

book, God is drawing and dragging to Jesus those He is giving salvation to in this age, the ones that He "made kings and priests." (Rev. 1:6) Paul continues in verse 8 saying if this "wisdom of God in a mystery" had been known by the powers in the world, they would not have crucified Jesus. What is that "mystery"? Paul speaks frequently of "the mystery" but does tell us what it is in Colossians 1:27, "To whom God would make known what is the riches of the glory of this mystery among the Gentiles; which is Christ in you, the hope of glory." If the powers had known and realized that the killing of one man, Jesus, would result in thousands being given the indwelling presence of the Holy Spirit with power and authority, doing the same works and greater works than Jesus did, they would never have killed Him. It was this mystery that God ordained, predetermined, or predestinated before the world, or ages, came into being.

## ROMANS 8:29-30

Let us now turn our attention to the verses that specifically speak of "predestinate" and "predestinated." We'll begin with the verses in the book of Romans. Many quote Romans 8:28, or at least the first part of the verse, "And we know that all things work together for good to them that love God, to them who are the called according to his purpose." Paul continues with verses 29 and 30, the two verses where we find *proorizo* used and translated "predestinate." "For whom he did foreknow, he also did predestinate to be conformed to the image of his Son, that he might be the firstborn among many brethren. Moreover whom he did predestinate, them he also called, and whom he called, them he also justified: and whom he justified, them he also glorified."

Paul says that God predestinated, predetermined, all of those He foreknew. Proponents of the most commonly taught "predestination doctrine" would have us believe that God ONLY knew beforehand that small group He decided to make into His sons. We looked a bit earlier at 1 Peter 1:20 where the exact same Greek word, *proginosko*, is used. In that passage it was speaking of Jesus being ordained, known beforehand, by God even before creation, that through His blood we would be given salvation. He KNEW that mankind would sin and would need a savior, a redeemer, and predetermined, premeditated, that He would send Jesus. Just as He FOREKNEW that He would send Jesus He FOREKNEW each of us and our need for redemption. If we question whether God knows us, has known us, from even before we WERE, please go and read Psalms 139. David states in verse 1 that God had known him. As he continues through the chapter, he recounts how God was there before he WAS, before his parents were aware of him, before God gave him life. These verses apply to each of us. God knew us from before we WERE. We are the "whom he did foreknow."

Paul says that God predetermined, predestinated, us to be conformed to the image of His son. The creation account in Genesis tells us that mankind was created in the "image and likeness" of God. It appears that that image and likeness was God's spiritual image and likeness. That was lost by Adam's sin, but God planned, predetermined, predestinated, that Jesus would come as our redeemer to conquer the adversary and bring salvation. Through that gift of salvation we, each one of us, would be brought to conformation to the image of His son, Jesus. Jesus was the firstborn, the firstfruits to be resurrected. And, notice it says the "firstborn among many brethren."

37

The word "many," translated from the Greek *polos*, Strong's number G4183, is defined as "much, many, large." However, it is used upon occasion to mean "ALL." Go with me to Romans 5. Let us read and comprehend verse 19, "For as by one man's disobedience many were made sinners, so by the obedience of one shall many be made righteous." I ask, how "many" became sinners? We are told that ALL have sinned and come short of the glory of God. (Rom. 3:23; Rom. 5:12) The "many" to be made righteous by the obedience of one (Jesus) is the same "many" that have sinned. "Many" here definitely means ALL.

I can almost hear some of you reading these verses with me saying that God hasn't called, justified and glorified ALL. "Have ye not read," as Jesus might say, God "calleth those things which be not as though they were." (Rom. 4:17) When God has determined something, it is accomplished, even IF we haven't seen it yet with our physical eyes. His word is sure. Just as surely as He predestinated ALL to be conformed to the image of His Son, He determined that He would call each one, that each would be justified, and ALL would be glorified. (We'll be looking at more of this in detail later in the book.)

In the context here, in verse 32, Paul states that God the Father didn't spare His Son, Jesus, but "delivered him up" for ALL OF US. With that absolute statement Paul asks a rhetorical question, "How shall he not with him also freely give us all things?" What things has he been speaking of? Calling, justifying, and glorifying, specifically! Paul concludes the chapter by telling us that he is persuaded that absolutely NOTHING can separate us from the love of God. And, how many of us did He love? John 3:16 says He loved the world, the whole world, all of mankind. He loved us enough to send His Son to die for each of us.

## EPHESIANS 1:5 AND 11

The final two verses in which Paul mentions "predestinated" are in the first chapter of the book of Ephesians. We'll quote them and then go back and look at them in context. Ephesians 1:5, "Having predestinated us unto the adoption of children by Jesus Christ to himself, according to the good pleasure of his will." Ephesians 1:11, "In whom also we have obtained an inheritance, being predestinated according to the purpose of him who worketh all things after the counsel of his own will."

The letter to the church of Ephesus was written by the apostle Paul. In verse 1 he addresses it to the saints at Ephesus and to the faithful in Christ. Coming to verse 4 he makes an important statement. Paul states that God "hath chosen us." And, notice that he states when this happened, "before the foundation of the world." Is this only the "saints at Ephesus" and the faithful few? Let us keep reading; Paul answers the question. Verse 5, quoted above, says that God predestinated, predetermined, that we would be adopted as children by Jesus Christ and that this was "according to the good pleasure of his will." Again, we ask, was it His will to ONLY adopt the few at Ephesus?

Paul praises God's grace in verse 6, "wherein he hath made us accepted in the beloved." As a side note, the Greek word translated "accepted" is the same word used in Luke 1:28, where Mary was told she was "highly favored." Who all is included in the "us" in this verse? Let us keep reading. In the next verse, verse 7, Paul continues and says that it is through Jesus "in whom we have redemption through his blood, the forgiveness of sins." Who is included in the "we"? Verse 8 again states that it is the "us" who God "hath abounded toward" in all wisdom and prudence. Paul speaks further of "us" in verse 9. He states that God has made known to "us" the "mystery of his will." That, he says, was "according to God's good pleasure which he hath purposed in himself."

Coming now to verse 10 we are given the answer to the "us" and the "we" that Paul has been referring to through this whole passage. Read this verse with me, "That in the dispensation of the fulness of times he might gather together in one **all things** in Christ, both which are in heaven, and which are on earth; even in him." (Emphasis mine.) Did you see that? **ALL** things, things referring not to rocks and trees but to people. Study the word translated all and you will find that it means, you guessed it, ALL. Paul's words in this passage, although being written to those at Ephesus, include ALL. ALL have been predestinated, predetermined, to be brought to adoption, to be redeemed, with our sins forgiven. We'll look at this in much more detail a bit later.

Verse 11, which was quoted above, continues the points made in verse 10. Paul states that the **ALL** that are to be gathered, including the "**we**," "will have obtained an inheritance" which was predestinated, predetermined, planned before, according "to the purpose of him (speaking of God) who worketh **ALL** things after the counsel of his will." The rest of this chapter is powerful, but let us take note specifically of verses 22 and 23, "And hath put **ALL** things under his feet, and gave him to be the head over **ALL** things to the church, which is his body, the fulness of him that filleth **ALL IN ALL**." (Emphasis mine.)

## NO RESPECT OF PERSONS

As we conclude this brief look at the teaching, belief, and doctrine of predestination, it seems once we get past the widely held beliefs of mankind's free will, and that this is the only day of salvation, the verses that have been the subject of debate become pretty clear. The belief that God has decided long ago that He would save some and send others to an eternity of torment and torture DOESN'T square with the numerous scriptures that tell us that with God there is no respect of persons.

Romans 2:11, "For there is no respect of persons with God." Ephesians 6:11, "neither is there respect of persons with him." Colossians 3:25, "and there is no respect of persons." What God plans for one He plans for ALL.

# CHAPTER FIVE

# WHAT ABOUT THE UNPARDONABLE SIN?

Many have heard the frightening words by the evangelist that they could be guilty of a sin so great and so devastating in its awfulness that the shed blood of Jesus Christ could not wash it away. This sin could never be forgiven, an unpardonable sin. They are told that the scriptures are there, that this sin does exist, and it is very possible they could sin such a horrendous sin. I ask, does such a sin exist, and if so, could you or I possibly have committed such a sin, or might we be in danger of committing it in the future?

## MATTHEW 12:22-32

Most who teach that there is such a sin will turn to a teaching given by Jesus. This teaching is recorded for us in two of the gospel accounts. Sadly, most who teach this doctrine have not taken the time to really study these accounts and harmonize them with all scriptures. Let us turn to Matthew's gospel and read what is recorded for us, Matthew 12:22-32. Let us look at the context and look at what Jesus said regarding the subject. When we go to the first few verses of the chapter, we find that the Pharisees accused Jesus and

His disciples of breaking the Sabbath by plucking a few heads of grain, rubbing out the kernels, and eating them. Following this encounter, Jesus and His disciples went into the synagogue, verse 9. We find that again the ones there asking questions to tempt Him were the Pharisees. After Jesus healed a man with a withered hand, the Pharisees went out and held a meeting, to discuss how they could destroy Jesus, verse 14.

In verse 15 we are told that the multitudes followed Jesus, and He healed them. Now we come to the account in which this "unpardonable" sin is discussed. After Jesus healed an individual who was possessed with a demon, verse 22, we find that the people, the multitudes, recognized Him as the son of David, the Messiah. Guess who was on the scene speaking against Jesus? You guessed it, the Pharisees, the major religious group. Notice in verse 24 what they were saying, "This fellow doth not cast out devils, but by Beelzebub the prince of the devils."

If you call to mind the numerous occasions we read of, you'll begin to notice that these guys had a perpetual fear that they might lose their hold on the people, and they were willing to do almost anything to keep the people from following Jesus. They were quite proud of their reputation. They knew that the people had been supporting their power, had been filling their purses. They knew that if Jesus' popularity and power continued to increase, they were going to lose everything they had. They had to admit that what had just taken place here, a demon possessed individual being healed of blindness and his inability to speak, involved something other than natural human power. Obviously they weren't going to admit that

Jesus was doing this by the power of God. So what did they do? They accused Him of doing it by the power of the devil.

Let us notice Jesus' response, verses 25-28, from the Amplified Version. "And knowing their thoughts, He said to them, Any kingdom that is divided against itself is being brought to desolation and laid waste, and no city or house divided against itself will last or continue to stand. And if Satan drives out Satan, he has become divided against himself and disunified; how then will his kingdom last or continue to stand? And if I drive out the demons by the help of Beelzebub, by whose help do your sons (the exorcists of the Jews) drive them out? For this reason they shall be your judges. But if it is by the Spirit of God that I drive out the demons, then the kingdom of God has come upon you before you expected it."

Now we come to the words with which the paragraph closes. Jesus addresses these words to these same self-righteous religious leaders of the Jewish nation. The solemn words that Jesus utters demand our attention. We need not place untrue emphasis on them, but neither do we need to minimize what He says. If we aren't careful, we can read into these words meanings He never intended, or we can explain away these most solemn words. Let us read these words, verses 31-33, from the King James Version, "All manner of sin and blasphemy shall be forgiven unto men: but the blasphemy against the Holy Ghost shall not be forgiven unto men. And whosoever speaketh a word against the Son of man, it shall be forgiven him: but whosoever speaketh against the Holy Ghost, it shall not be forgiven him, neither in this world, neither in the world to come."

What is the sin against the Holy Spirit? We find the parallel account to what we have just read here in Matthew 12 over in Mark the third chapter, verses 22-30.

# MARK 3:22-30

Let us look at verses 28-30 of Mark 3 in the King James Version. "Verily I say unto you, All sins shall be forgiven unto the sons of men, and blasphemies wherewith soever they shall blaspheme: But he that shall blaspheme against the Holy Ghost hath never forgiveness, but is in danger of eternal damnation. **Because they said, He hath an unclean spirit.**" (Emphasis mine.) We get a clue here. The opposition the Pharisees had toward Jesus wasn't just a spur of the moment thing. It is obvious that they knew what they were doing and saying. Remember the story of Nicodemus, a Pharisee who came to Jesus at night. He told Jesus, John 3:2, "Rabbi, we know that thou art a teacher come from God: for no man can do these miracles that thou doest, except God be with him." Many of these Pharisees, if not most, knew better but still plotted to destroy Jesus. Jesus presented a threat to their position and power over the people. Jesus warned them of the consequences of their attitude and actions. Their sin was not against God in heaven or the Son of God on earth. They were resisting, opposing, and attacking the Holy Spirit, the very activity and administration of God toward them. Jesus warned them that they were in danger of blaspheming the Holy Spirit.

We often think of the Holy Spirit as "power," and certainly there is power, but perhaps it might be better viewed as "force," God's energy force, by which He accomplishes His purpose and executes His will. As we look at what was going on, we see that these religious leaders were not in danger of committing this sin because they said Jesus was performing His miracles by the power of the devil. Jesus said that could be forgiven. They were expressing an attitude of unbelief which was a calculated rejection of the activity of God toward them. They were resisting the Holy Spirit. Notice what Stephen said to these same Pharisees right before he was stoned. Acts 7:51, "Ye stiffnecked and uncircumcised in heart and ears, ye do always resist the Holy Ghost."

As we just looked at in these passages, Jesus was not addressing His disciples nor the people who came to hear Him and to receive healing. He was speaking directly to the Pharisees, the leaders of the Jewish nation. Jesus stated that He came to His own, His own people and nation, and "his own received him not." (John 1:11) His statements were directed at the Jewish nation, specifically the religious leaders. He was not directing His words to you and me. Blasphemy against the Holy Spirit was serious. It was greater than speaking against the Father or Jesus. These same people, the leaders, were the ones who trumped up the charges against Him and had Him crucified. But, for all of that they were forgiven. Luke 23:34 records for us Jesus' prayer to the Father, "Father, forgive them; for they know not what they do."

Let us read again His statement in Matthew 12:31, "All manner of sin and blasphemy shall be forgiven unto men." Jesus says ALL. The Greek word is *pas*, Strong's number G3956. It is defined as a primary word meaning "all, any, every, the whole, each, everyone, all things, everything." Of the 1238 times this word is used, it is translated "all" 975 times. It means ALL. It means that there IS NO UNPARDONABLE SIN. So, how do we reconcile the rest of the verse?

Let us read again what Jesus said, "but the blasphemy against the Holy Ghost shall not be forgiven unto men." (Matt. 12:32) Let's not stop here. In verse 32 Jesus says, "it shall not be forgiven him, neither in this world, neither in the world to come." Jesus adds some additional information here. He says the forgiveness to men is "not" in "this world" or in "the world to come." What is He saying?

## NEITHER IN THIS WORLD, NEITHER IN THE WORLD TO COME.

The King James Version of the Bible we have been quoting says "neither in this world, neither in the world to come." However, that isn't quite the meaning of the Greek. The Greek word that is translated here as "world" is *aion*, Strong's number G165. The definition is "properly an age." The duration of an "age" is indefinite but does have an ending. If the translators had used the correct word "age" instead of "world" much confusion could have been avoided. Several other translations have corrected this. Here are a few: "Whoever may speak against the Holy Spirit, it shall not be forgiven him, neither in this age, nor in that which is coming." (Young's Literal Translation) The Weymouth New Testament renders this as, "Whoever speaks against the Holy Spirit shall obtain forgiveness neither in this age or in the age to come." One of the most popular translations, The New International Version, renders it, "Anyone who speaks against the Holy Spirit will not be forgiven either in this age or in the age to come." The English Standard Versions says, "but whoever speaks against the Holy Spirit will not be forgiven, either in this age or in the age to come." Jesus was plainly telling these individuals that forgiveness would not come in the age they were living in, nor would it come in the next age. He leaves it to be understood based on His statement that all sin would be forgiven, that in an age to follow those two, forgiveness would be given. (Note: We can assume Jesus was speaking of the age of Law, this age, and the church age, the age to come. Nowhere are we told how many ages there may be, when they begin, nor when they end.)

If we are honest with the scripture, we can plainly see that Jesus' words do not prove nor proclaim that there is an unpardonable sin. First, He says ALL MANNER of sin and blasphemy shall be forgiven unto men. Secondly, He states that some sins could be forgiven in the age they were living in. He then states, thirdly, that other sins against the Holy Spirit could not be forgiven in the age when Jesus came to earth, nor in the age to immediately follow. These words clearly indicate that sins not forgiven in those two ages will be forgiven in the following age. There is absolutely nothing about a sin that is "unpardonable" throughout endless ages to come.

Before we conclude this chapter, let us go one more time to Mark 3. Verse 29 says, "But he that shall blaspheme against the Holy Ghost hath never forgiveness, but is in danger of eternal damnation." The concluding phrase, "but is in danger of eternal damnation," needs to be looked at briefly. Several things again bring confusion. The word "eternal" is most often believed to be "never ending," "without end." It is from *aionios*, in the Greek, Strong's number

G166. It, as you can probably see by looking at the word, is derived from *aion* which we just looked at. It means "age during" or "age lasting." A correct rendering of "damnation" would be "judgment." This verse from the original should be rendered "has not for the eon (age) forgiveness, but is in danger of eonian (age-during) judgment." This gives a much different meaning. The Emphatic Diaglott has it, "But whoever may blaspheme against the Holy Spirit, has no forgiveness to the age, but is exposed to Aionian Judgment."

Although we won't pursue it in this book, it appears that Jesus was telling these leaders of the Jewish people that they would not, as a nation, receive His salvation until after that age and the then coming age were past. Paul tells us that "all Israel shall be saved," Romans 11:26. But, he said just prior to those words, verse 25, that it wouldn't be "until the fulness of the Gentiles be come in." He was aware of Jesus' statement that it would be after the two ages He addressed. Perhaps his statement helps us understand the statement that "the last shall be first and the first last." (Matt. 20:16) Israel were the chosen, the ones Jesus came to, the ones who were to be first. In their rejection the Gentiles, who would have been last, became the first.

Once we look at what Jesus actually said, we can rejoice that there is no sin that won't be forgiven. There is no sin that God the Father and Jesus won't forgive, no sin that Jesus' blood doesn't cover.

# CHAPTER SIX

# WHAT ABOUT
# "UNIVERSALISM?"

The belief in universal salvation is as old as Christianity itself. Do a search on the internet and one will find much that has been written against this belief, but there is much also that presents it in a very positive way. Universalism is also referred to as "universal reconciliation," "universal salvation," and "Christian universalism." Many statements are made by those addressing the doctrine as being totally false. One writer states that Universalists attempt to make a doctrine from one or two verses (which is untrue) and thus "we know that the universalist teaching cannot be true." Some even title their writings or papers "The False Doctrine of Universalism." There are a few works that do look at this with objectivity.

One of the first works I read as I studied through what my friend had been attempting to show me was written in 1899 by J. W. Hanson. He put forth a great amount of proof (although discounted by many) that universal salvation was the prevailing doctrine of the early church.[2] Mr. Hanson cites many early Christian writers and teachers that held to the belief that all would be brought to salvation, including Clement of Alexandria and Origen. An extensive work, although quite scholarly, was published in 2013. Titled The Christian Doctrine of *Apokatastasis,* it was 16 years in research and writing and is approximately 900 pages in length. The author is Ilaria Ramelli Ph.D.[3] She has been Professor of Roman Near East History, an Assistant in Ancient Philosophy (Catholic University, since 2003). She has a long list of other credentials. If you are wondering, *Apokatastasis* is a transliteration of a Greek word that means "restoration." Apokatastasis involves a belief in universal salvation.

I have not read all 900 pages of this work. However, here are a couple of reviews by some that have. "This deeply impressive study is the fruit of sixteen years of research into the history of early Christian belief in universal salvation. In almost 900 pages of carefully argued analysis, Ramelli leaves no stone unturned in her attempt to recover a story that has never before been told with anything like this much attention to the range and depth of evidence." (Robin A. Parry, International Journal of Systematic Theology) "The most definitive account of the oft-controversial Christian version of the doctrine of the apokatastasis, or restoration/reintegration/reconstitution – and will probably remain such for a considerable time ... a

---

[2] J. W. Hanson Universalism The Prevailing Doctrine Of The Christian Church During Its First Five Hundred Years

Download as PDF www.mercyuponall.org/wp-content/uploads/2015/02/Prevailing.pdf

[3] Ilaria Ramelli The Christian Doctrine of Apokatastasis

Download as PDF https://afkimel.files.wordpress.com/2021/08/the-christian-doctrine-of-apokatastasis-b-ilaria-l.e.-ramelli-.pdf

jewel in the crown of books on Patristics, Early Christian Studies, and Christian Philosophy ... a book that cuts to the very core of theological thought, dialogue, controversy in early Christianity. Highly recommended." (Chris L. De Wet, Journal of Early Christian History)

A question regarding *apokatastasis* was addressed on the website gotquestions.org.[4] A couple of statements were made that I would like to share. "Apocatastasis was taught early on by Gregory of Nyssa, Clement of Alexandria, and Origen. Later, it was a belief held by the Moravian Brethren, the Christadelphians, and many Anabaptists." "The doctrine of apocatastasis was condemned as heresy at the Second Council of Constantanople in AD 553. Apocatastasis was also opposed by Augustine, Jerome, and Luther, and it has never been widely taught within most Christian traditions."

## ULTIMATE RECONCILIATION AND SALVATION OF ALL

I like to refer to what our friends were attempting to show us in 1999, and with what I came to see from my studies, as the ultimate reconciliation and salvation of ALL. As I looked at what is currently being taught by the various adherents to universalism, I found a number of beliefs that I couldn't (and still can't) agree with. I'll mention a few as we continue.

The most extreme and actually "non-Christian" of those that hold to a universalist belief is the Unitarian Universalist Association.

---

[4] www.gotquestions.org/apocatastasis.html

Although the website wikipedia may not always be reliable, what they tell us fits with what UUA state on their own website. I quote first from wikipedia.[5] "UUA is a liberal religious association of Unitarian Universalist congregations. It was formed in 1961 by the consolidation of the American Unitarian Association and the Universalist Church of America, both Protestant Christian denominations with Unitarian and Universalist doctrines, respectively. However, modern Unitarian Universalists see themselves as a separate religion with its own beliefs and affinities. They define themselves as non-creedal, and draw wisdom from various religions and philosophies, including humanism, pantheism, Christianity, Hinduism, Buddhism, Taoism, Judaism, Islam, and earth-centered spirituality. Thus the UUA is a syncretistic religious group with liberal leanings."

Here are a few things from the Unitarian Universalist Association's (UUA) own website.[6] "Every individual should be encouraged to develop a personal philosophy of life." "We do not need any other person, official, or organization to tell us what to believe." "Truth is not absolute; it changes over time." "We have no specific doctrines to which members are expected to subscribe." "We do not have a defined doctrine of God. Members are free to develop individual concepts of God that are meaningful to them. They are also free to reject the term and concept altogether."

Despite all this, the stated beliefs of the Universalist Church appear to come much closer to what is seen in the Holy Scriptures. They look to many of the same scriptures I will be sharing with you

---

[5] https://en.wikipedia.org/wiki/Unitarian_Universalist_Association
[6] https://www.uusg.org/what-is-a-uu

in the next chapter. I do see some differences. Here are a few things from their website.[7] "The sentiment by which Universalists are distinguished, is this: *that at last every individual of the human race shall become holy and happy.*" "An attempt has been recently made to distinguish Universalists only by a disbelief in future punishment. Such an attempt is unjustifiable. They agree in the great doctrine of the *final holiness and happiness of all men* and they leave every man to form his own opinion in regard to the times and seasons when this great event shall transpire." They discuss various individuals that had differing beliefs, some believing in future punishment and others who didn't. Their final statement after discussing these various beliefs was this, "*All persons are Universalists who truly believe in the salvation of all mankind through grace of the Lord Jesus Christ.*"

As we have touched on earlier, the Bible does tell us of future punishment, the spiritual fire that is used to purify. It is punish**ment**, not punish**ing** for all eternity. It is corrective. It is chastening. The writer of the book of Hebrews gave us insight into what God works through His chastening, the punishment He will bring. Let us read these words, Hebrews 12:6-11. "For whom the LORD loveth he chasteneth, and scourgeth every son he receiveth. If ye endure chastening, God dealth with you as with sons; for what son is he whom the father chasteneth not? But if ye be without chastisement, whereof all are partakers, then are ye bastards, and not sons. Furthermore we have had fathers of our flesh which corrected us, and we gave them reverence: shall we not much rather be in subjection unto

---

7 . http://www.christianuniversalism.net/universalist-theology/the-plain-guide-to-universalism-by-thomas-whittemore-1840/what- do-universalists-believe/index.html

the Father of spirits, and live? For they verily for a few days chastened us after their own pleasure; but he for our profit, that we might be partakers of his holiness. Now no chastening for the present seemeth to be joyous, but grievous: nevertheless afterward it yieldeth the peaceable fruit of righteousness unto them which are exercised thereby."

In the next chapter, we will look at many of the numerous scriptures, that reveal God's plan from before the creation to reconcile and save ALL who have ever had life. He knew mankind's frame and proclivity. He made the serpent and gave him a job to do. (Obtain my book **AN EXPOSE´ OF THE ADVERSARY** for greater understanding of this.) He designed a wonderful plan where each and every one would be dealt with, their fallen nature and will would be changed, and their belief in and confession of Jesus as savior would result. What a glorious plan that most of us have never seen nor heard!

# CHAPTER SEVEN

# DOES GOD PLAN TO RECONCILE AND SAVE ALL?

In this chapter I will share with you some of the numerous scriptures that reveal God's glorious plan for mankind. Most of us have read over these passages without comprehending what we are being told. As pointed out earlier, many commonly held beliefs have kept us from seeing what is right in front of us. I often quote Proverbs 25:2, "It is the glory of God to conceal a thing: but the honour of kings to search out a matter." We are told that He has made us kings and priests unto God and his Father." (Rev.1:6) So, as kings we are honored to search out what God has planned and prepared for all of mankind. Let us begin our search.

## 1 TIMOTHY 2:3-4

"For this is good and acceptable in the sight of God our Saviour; Who will have all men to be saved, and to come unto the knowledge of the truth." (1 Tim. 2:3-4) The apostle Paul, writing to the evangelist Timothy, begins this chapter with an exhortation to pray for all men. He then tells him what we just quoted, still regarding all men. What does he say about ALL men? In verse 4 we read of God "who will." This word is translated from the Greek word *thelo*, Strong's number G2309. Thayer's Greek Definitions gives the following as the meanings of this Greek word, "to will, have in mind, intend, to be resolved or determined, to purpose." This isn't stating that God just sort of had a passing whim that it might be nice if all could be saved. No! It states dogmatically that it is His will, His desire, that He had in His mind, that He intended, that He was resolved and determined, and it was His purpose that ALL men be saved.

We looked at the Greek word translated "all" earlier. The Greek word is *pas*, Strong's number G3956. And, as we pointed out earlier it means ALL, not just some or a few. It leaves out no one. It seems pretty definite that God has willed, intended, planned, and purposed to bring ALL of mankind to salvation and to come to know His truth. Remember, Jesus is the truth! Once again let us take a quick look at Job 42:2 from the English Standard Version, "I know you can do all things, and that no purpose of yours can be thwarted." What God has purposed will come to pass.

Before we move on from 1 Timothy 2 let us look at verse 6, "Who gave himself a ransom for all, to be testified in due time." Speaking of Jesus (verse 5), we are told that through His death on the cross He paid the ransom for ALL. We have all been "kidnapped" by the adversary. Jesus' life, being worth more than the combined worth of all of mankind, was given in payment for the ransom. As the ones kidnapped, we had no part in that payment being made.

58

This was the plan made before creation, that Jesus would come and die to ransom us, to redeem us. How many did He pay the ransom for? Read it again, "for ALL." None were left out. He didn't pay the ransom for just a few but for ALL. This will be testified to in due time.

## 2 PETER 3:9

Peter is reminding his readers, including us, of the many things spoken by God's prophets and apostles. He speaks of the last days, 2 Pet. 3:3. He speaks of scoffers that ask when is He going to come? They seem to believe things continue as they were. Verse 5 states that these individuals are willingly ignorant of all that has taken place. Peter tells these individuals, verse 8, not to be ignorant of one thing, a day with God is as a thousand years and a thousand years are as a day. We now come to verse 9, "The LORD is not slack concerning his promise, as some men count slackness; but is longsuffering to us-ward, **not willing that any should perish, but that all should come to repentance.**" (Emphasis mine.) The word translated "willing" is from the Greek *boulomai*, Strong's number G1014. It compares to number G2309, *thelo*, that we looked at earlier. The word is defined as "to will deliberately, have a purpose, be minded." Peter states that God is NOT WILLING that any should perish. He states that God wills that ALL, the same all from the Greek *pas,* should come to repentance. When God wills that none perish, that ALL come to repentance, He will see that it happens.

Sadly, many try to get around this very plain statement. One man who has been in ministry for many years, made the following comment about this verse. "This clearly states that it is not the LORD'S will for anyone to perish, but people are perishing." A couple of sentences further on he says, "Relatively few people are saved compared to the number that are lost. God's will for people concerning salvation is not being accomplished." How sad. This is akin to blasphemy, saying that God is not accomplishing what He has proposed to do. This is just as Peter stated, some would say God is slack concerning His promise. What I believe the problem is with this man (and many others) is that he believes today is the only day of salvation. True, many are not being saved today. But, as we have looked at in this book, God has a plan worked out for all to have their day of salvation.

Verse 15 of this chapter states, "And account that the longsuffering of our LORD is salvation." As verse 9 says, God "is longsuffering to us-ward." Peter explains here in verse 15 that the longsuffering toward us is salvation.

# ROMANS 5:19

We looked at Romans 5:19 earlier in Chapter Four of this book, but let us look at it again. "For as by one man's disobedience many were made sinners, so by the obedience of one shall many be made righteous." What we see here is an equation. On one side of the equation is "the many made sinners." On the other side of the equation is "the many made righteous." Paul had said the same thing in different words back in verse 15. Again he is making an equation. Notice. "For if through the offence of one "many be dead," (the one side of the equation) "the gift of grace, which is by one man, Jesus Christ, hath abounded unto many." (the other side of the equation) In an equation both sides are equal. The number of sinners (all have sinned) equals the number of righteous (all will be made righteous). The "many" that are dead equals the "many" that the grace of Jesus Christ abounds to. **All** (the many in these verses) that were made sinners and that "be dead" are the many, the **all**, that are made righteous and have Jesus' grace extended to them. Paul declares that **ALL** have sinned and have come short of the glory of God, and the same **ALL** will receive God's righteousness through the grace of Jesus Christ. (Rom. 3:23)

We just referenced Romans 3:23 above but let us take a quick look at it and the following verse, verse 24. Verse 23, "For all have sinned, and come short of the glory of God." Continuing on with verse 24 Paul states these same ALL are "being justified freely by his grace through the redemption that is in Christ Jesus." Paul, over and over, shows God's glorious plan to bring reconciliation and salvation to ALL of mankind.

## SAVIOUR OF THE WORLD

Jesus said, "for I came not to judge the world, but to save the world." (John 12:47) The word "world" is translated from the Greek word *kosmos*, Strong's number G2889. It has a number of meanings depending on context, but it is apparent here that it means "the inhabitants of the earth, men, the human family." What did Jesus say He came to earth to do? "But to save the world," the inhabitants of the earth, men, the human family. He included ALL inhabitants of the earth. Did He "save the world" or not? The last words He spoke on the cross before breathing His last was, in English, "it is finished." He finished, accomplished, what He came to do. ALL were saved. We may not see it with our eyes but He calls "those things which be not as though they were." (Rom. 4:17)

This passage in John 12 is not the only place Jesus is referred to as Saviour. In chapter 4 of John we have recorded for us the encounter Jesus had with the woman of Samaria at the well. After His comments to her she returned to the city and told many others of Jesus. In verses 41 and 42 we find that a large number from the city came to see and hear from Jesus. It tells us, "And many more believed because of his own word; And said unto the woman, Now we believe, not because of thy saying: for we have heard him ourselves, and know that this is indeed the Christ, the Saviour of the world." Jesus didn't correct them or tell them that He wasn't the Saviour, even though He remained there for two more days. (verse 43) He was come to "save the world." That was what He did, and Saviour was who He was, the Saviour of the world, the whole world. He didn't just manage to save a few.

Let us look at words penned by the apostle John, 1 John 4:14, "And we have seen and do testify that the Father sent the Son to be the Saviour of the world." Yes, the Father sent Jesus to save the world, to be the Saviour of the world. Jesus accomplished the job He came to earth to do. Jesus saved the world, the whole world, all of the world, all the inhabitants (past, present, and future) of the *kosmos*. There were none excluded. There weren't some that managed to escape being saved.

When Jesus came, He was given power and authority to accomplish what He came to do. Prior to His crucifixion Jesus said, "And I, if I be lifted up from the earth, will draw ALL men unto me." (John 12:32) The next verse tells us He spoke this in reference to the death He would experience. We know that it is no longer an "if" He be lifted up, but instead a definite "He was crucified." His word is sure. He said that He would draw, or drag, ALL men to Him. The Bible in Basic English renders this "will make all men come to me." Jesus is the Saviour of the world.

## EPHESIANS 1:10

We discussed some of these verses here in the first chapter of the letter to the Ephesians when we looked at predestination. Picking up the account in verses 9 and 10 we read, "Having made known unto us the mystery of his will, according to his good pleasure which he has purposed in himself: that in the dispensation of the fulness of times he might gather together in one ALL things in Christ, both which are in heaven, and which are on earth; even in him." "All things" is translated from the Greek word *pas* that we defined earlier. It is speaking of people, not rocks or animals. It says "ALL," not some, not a few, not even most, but ALL.

## PHILIPPIANS 2:9-11

Most of us have read these words Paul wrote to the church at Philippi without even grasping what he is saying. Let us read them together. "Wherefore God also hath highly exalted him, and given him a name which is above every name: That at the name of Jesus every knee should bow, of things in heaven, and things in earth, and things under the earth; And that every tongue should confess that Jesus Christ is LORD, to the glory of God the Father." The word "thing" in these verses is in italics, indicating it isn't translated from any Greek word. It is understood that it is speaking of people. Other translations make that plain. The Greek word rendered into English as "every" is *pas*, translated as ALL in many of the verses we have looked at. We are finding the same reference to "all" and "every" person or individual.

I believe we should go back to the words of God written down by the prophet Isaiah, Isaiah 45:21-23, beginning in the middle of verse 21, "and there is no God else beside me; a just God and a Saviour; there is none beside me. Look unto me, and be ye saved, all ends of the earth: for I am God, and there is none else. I have sworn by myself, the word is gone out of my mouth in righteousness, and shall not return, That unto me every knee shall bow, every tongue shall swear." God says He is Saviour. He tells the whole world to look unto Him and be saved. He dogmatically says that **every** knee shall bow, **every** tongue shall swear. There is no room for argument. His WORD is absolute. When He says every knee shall bow it is to be in heart-felt adoration and worship. It isn't, as I have heard a few proclaim, that even if God has to break their legs they will bow. NO, NO, NO! He will, as Saviour, bring ALL to salvation, He will have ALL to be saved. Notice again verse 22, "Look unto me, and be ye saved."

Going back to Philippians chapter 2 we easily see that Paul is quoting God's words from Isaiah 45. If you care to check, Paul also quoted these words in his letter to the Romans, Rom. 14:11. Paul knew, and tells us, that it is impossible for one to confess that Jesus is LORD and Saviour without God's Holy Spirit. "Wherefore I give you to understand, that no man speaking by the Spirit of God calleth Jesus accursed: and that no man can say that Jesus is the LORD, but by the Holy Ghost." (1 Cor. 12:3) Having our legs broken or forced at gunpoint to say we confess is not true confession. Paul tells us it has to be by God's Holy Spirit. Paul knew God's plan. He knew that ultimately ALL would be reconciled to God and given salvation.

## HEBREWS 8:11-12

Here in chapter 8 of the book of Hebrews the writer is speaking of the new covenant, a better covenant (verse 6). Beginning in verse 8 the author quotes from the prophet Jeremiah, Jeremiah 31:31-34. In verse 10-12 we read what that new covenant was to contain, "For this is the covenant that I will make with the house of Israel after those days, saith the LORD; I will put my laws into their mind, and write them in their hearts: and I will be to them a God, and they shall be to me a people: And they shall not teach every man his neighbor, and every man his brother, saying, Know the LORD: for all shall know me, from the least to the greatest. For I will be merciful to their unrighteousness, and their sins and their iniquities will I remember no more." In verse 11 God is saying "every man," translated from the Greek *hekastos*, Strong's number G1538, which means "each, every," will have no need to be taught by his neighbor or his brother. Why? Because, He says ALL, the Greek word *pas* again, will know Him. He will have "drawn" each and every one, and each and every one will have had their nature, their will, changed. Obviously they will have been given the faith for salvation and been granted repentance, as He says all of the sins and iniquities are forgiven and forgotten. ALL will ultimately be included in that new covenant. ALL will know God and Jesus. ALL will have God's law in their minds and on their hearts. ALL will receive reconciliation and salvation.

Continuing in verse 13 the author reveals that the old covenant was obsolete, the new covenant was established and the ALL mentioned in verse 11 were to be included under it. God's plan is to include ALL. Praise God for what He is working out in His perfect timing.

# LUKE 3:6

Luke in his account of the life and ministry of Jesus Christ begins telling us of the ministry of John the Baptist here in chapter 3 of his gospel. In verses 1 and 2 he gives the time setting. In verse 3 he begins to tell us of John. Luke then quotes from the prophet Isaiah, Isaiah 40:3-5. His wording is slightly different from what Jeremiah wrote. Luke, in verse 4 quotes Isaiah, "The voice of one crying in the wilderness, Prepare ye the way of the LORD, make his paths straight."(Isa. 40:3) Following the same format of Isaiah's prophecy in verses 4-5 of Isaiah 40, Luke speaks of the ultimate result of Jesus' ministry and His Work. Luke even gives a bit more for us. Let us compare the two accounts.

Isaiah 40:4-5, "Every valley shall be exalted, and every mountain and hill shall be made low: and the crooked shall be made straight, and the rough places plain: And the glory of the LORD shall be revealed, and all flesh shall see it together: for the mouth of the LORD hath spoken it." Now, Luke 3:5 and 6, "Every valley shall be filled, and every mountain and hill shall be brought low; and the crooked shall be made straight, and the rough ways shall be made smooth; And all flesh shall see the salvation of God." Did you notice the main difference? Isaiah said that "all flesh" would see the glory of God together. Luke says "all flesh" will see the salvation of God. Obviously God's salvation is God's glory!

Let us look at what Luke is telling us in a bit more detail. When he says "all flesh" he is using a phrase used throughout the Bible to indicate "all human beings." In Genesis 7:21 the term is used to indicate the whole population of the earth, other than Noah and his family, was destroyed in the flood. In that verse a bit more information was given to show that there it even included animal "flesh."

Luke states that ALL flesh, all of mankind, would "see" the salvation of God. Some have tried to explain this by stating that even those that supposedly were in hell would be able to look up on the saved and thus see His salvation. The word "see" as used by Luke means more than that. The Greek word translated "see" is *optomai*, Strong's number G3700. Checking on this word we find that it is used as the future of *horao*, Strong's number G3708. A definition of *optomai* is "to truly comprehend." Looking at the definitions of *horah* we find something very interesting, "by Hebraism to experience."

Luke is clearly telling us that "ALL flesh," ALL of mankind will SEE, by experiencing, the salvation of God.

# Colossians 1:20

In Paul's letter "to the saints and faithful brethren" at Colosse he speaks of God's "dear Son," Jesus, and records for us that ALL things were created by Him (verse 16, chapter 1). He emphasizes this by stating it two times and saying that the ALL included both visible and invisible, thrones, dominions, and powers, that exist on earth and in heaven. In verse 17 he states that before Him and by Him ALL things consist. Leading up to verse 20 we see the statement regarding ALL (the Greek *pas*) three times. Now we come to verse 20, "And having made peace through the blood of his cross. By him to reconcile ALL things unto himself; by him, I say, whether they be things in earth, or things in heaven." We may not see with our physical eyes but as we read earlier in Romans 4:17, He "calleth those things which be not as though they were." It is a sure thing that ALL will be reconciled to God and His Son, Jesus. It is interesting to note in the next verse, verse 21, Paul addresses specifically the individuals in Colosse and says, "And YOU, that were sometime alienated and enemies in your mind by wicked works, yet NOW hath he reconciled." The process of reconciling ALL is now underway.

# John 17:2

John chapter 17 is a record of Jesus' prayer to the Father on the night He had the last supper with His apostles. In verse 1 He addresses His prayer to His Father and states that His hour, the time of His trial had come. He asked the Father to glorify Him and that He, the Son, might glorify the Father. Now, let us notice verse 2, "As thou hast given him power over all flesh, that he should give eternal life to as many as thou hast given him." The question we need to ask is "how many did the Father give Him?" If we know that we will know how many that Jesus will be giving eternal life to. Back a few chapters we read the answer, John 3:35, "The Father loveth the Son, and hath given ALL things into his hand." ALL have been given. Jesus said in the verse we just read, John 17:2, that he should give eternal life to as many, ALL, that the Father had given Him.

However, you may be asking about the next verse in John 3, verse 36. It states that "he that believeth not the Son shall not see life; but the wrath of God abidith on him." Wrath is defined as "punishment," correction. We looked earlier at the "fire of God" that purifies, that brings correction. This is what will "abide" on those that believed not. They won't see "life" until the process is complete. This statement in no way cancels out the clear scriptures that ALL are given into Jesus' hand and that ALL will be given eternal life.

## ROMANS 11:25-26

Because this chapter is becoming quite long, we'll look at only a couple more passages. There are many more that you can search out if you are interested.

In Romans chapter 11 Paul is speaking to Gentiles, verse 13. He speaks of branches being broken off and branches being grafted in. We won't go into a detailed discussion of this but let us drop down to verse 25, "For I would not, brethren, that ye should be ignorant of this mystery, lest ye should be wise in your own conceits; that blindness in part is happened to Israel, until the fulness of the Gentiles be come in." He is telling them he doesn't wish them to be ignorant of this "mystery." What is this mystery? He tells them, and us, that "blindness in part is happened to Israel." We won't go back over it but we discussed briefly in Chapter Five the sin against the Holy Spirit and that Jesus said there would not be forgiveness in "this age" nor "the age to come." Paul is saying that "blindness" has happened to Israel. He goes on to show that there will be an age in which the blindness will be removed. When will that be? Notice the last part of the verse, "until the fulness of the Gentiles be come in."

"Fulness" is from the Greek word *pleroma*, Strong's number G4138. It means "completion, full, fullness, filled up, completeness." Paul is stating that Israel will have the blindness removed once ALL the Gentiles have been dealt with. Then, notice what happens, verse 26, "And so ALL Israel shall be saved:" We once again have the Greek word *pas* being used here, the word that means ALL. Not a part, or some, or a few, BUT Paul tells us that ALL of Israel SHALL BE SAVED. We should read the last part of verse 26, "as it is written, There shall come out of Sion the Deliverer, and shall turn away ungodliness from Jacob." Ungodliness turned away indicates there will be GODLINESS. Godliness in ALL Israel states that ALL are saved!

# 1 CORINTHIANS 15:20-28

The nine verses we are going to look at contain a wealth of understanding of God's wonderful plan of salvation. We have read over it so many times without grasping what it is really telling us. Let us read the passage.

1 Corinthians 15:20-28, "But now is Christ risen from the dead, and become the firstfruits of them that slept. For since by man came death, by man came also the resurrection of the dead. For as in Adam all die, even so in Christ shall all be made alive. But every man in his own order: Christ the firstfruits; afterward they that are Christ's at his coming. Then cometh the end, when he shall have delivered up the kingdom to God, even the Father; when he shall have put down all rule and all authority and power. For he must reign, till he hath put all enemies under his feet. The last enemy that shall be destroyed is death. For he hath put all things under his feet. But when he saith all things are put under him, it is manifest that he is excepted, which did put all things under him. And when all things shall be subdued unto him, then shall the Son also himself be subject unto him that put all things under him, that God may be all in all."

Let us go back through these verses and notice a few things. My notes are in italics within brackets.

1 Corinthians 15:20, "But now is Christ risen from the dead, and become the firstfruits (*probably best rendered in the singular "firstfruit." Vine's Expository Dictionary of Biblical Words says, "Though the English word is plural in each of its occurrences save Rom. 11:16, the Greek word is always singular."*) of them that slept." (*the dead*)

1 Corinthians 15:21, "For since by man (*referring to Adam*) came death, by man (*referring to Jesus*) came also (*Strong's number G2532, kai in the Greek, can be rendered as also, even, likewise*) the resurrection of the dead."

1 Corinthians 15:22, "For as in Adam all (*ALL, every individual that has lived*) die, even (*same G2532, kai, also, even, likewise.*) so in Christ shall all (*ALL, every individual that has lived.*) be made alive."

1 Corinthians 15:23, "But every man (*every man, all men, ALL individuals, without exceptions*) in his own order: (*not all at one time but over a period of time. Strong's concordance defines this word, tama, Number G5001, "From G5021; something orderly in arrangement, that is, [figuratively] a series or succession:"*) Christ the firstfruits; (*He is first in the order of those made alive.*) afterward they that are Christ's at his coming. (*Those that are made alive at Jesus' coming are the second in order. What about the rest of the "every man"? Keep reading!*)

1 Corinthians 15:24, "Then cometh the end, (*What does he mean, the end. The Greek is "telos," number G5056 in Strong's. Notice the definition from the Lexicon: "termination, the limit at which a thing ceases to be (always of the end of some act or state, but not of the end of a period of time)." In other words at the end of the work Jesus commences at His return.*) when he shall have delivered up the kingdom to God, even the Father; (*The rest of the dead will be made alive before this occurs.*) when he shall have put down (*put down is Strong's number G2673, katargeo, meaning per the lexicon, to render idle, unemployed, inactivate, inoperative.*) all rule and all authority and power." (*All opposing His Kingdom.*)

1 Corinthians 15:25, "For he must reign, till (*Strong's number G891, achri, means until. Jesus doesn't reign forever, His rule comes to*

*an end. When does it end? Read on.*) he hath put all (***ALL***, *every one.*) enemies under his feet."

1 Corinthians 15:26, "The last enemy that shall be destroyed is death." (*How is death destroyed? All will be made alive, verse 22. The word 'destroyed' is Strong's number G2673, katargeo, that was translated 'put down' in verse 24 above. The meaning again is 'to render idle, unemployed, inactivate, inoperative.' There will be no more death.*)

1 Corinthians 15:27, "For he (*God the Father*) hath put (*see note below.*) all things (*ALL things is not talking about trees and rocks but ALL people.*) under (*see note below.*) his (Jesus') feet. But when he (*God the Father*) saith all things (*ALL people*) are put under (*see note below.*) him, (*Jesus*) it is manifest that he (*God the Father*) is excepted, which did put (*see note below.*) all things (*Again, ALL people, all that have ever lived.*) under (*see note below.*) him." (*Jesus*) (*NOTE: The words "put," "under," and "put under" used in this verse are from the Greek hupotasso, Strong's number G5293. The lexicon states that "In a non-military use, it was 'a voluntary attitude of giving in, cooperating, assuming responsibility, and carrying a burden."*)

1 Corinthians 15:28, "And when all things (*There it is again, ALL individuals.*) shall be subdued (*This is G5293 again that was translated 'put,' 'put under,' and 'under' in the previous verse.*) unto him, (*Jesus*) then shall the Son also himself be subject (*This also is G5293, a voluntary act.*) unto him (*God the Father*) that put (G5293 again.*) all things (*Once more we see ALL things, ALL people, ALL individuals.*) under (*Under is from G5293 again.*) him, (*Jesus*) that

God may be all in all." (*Can we grasp this? God will be ALL in ALL. Ultimate reconciliation and salvation for ALL.*)

Perhaps it will help to try and paraphrase these verses. The following is the "Pifer Paraphrase" of 1 Corinthians 15:20-28.

Verse 20, "But now Jesus is risen, resurrected, from the dead, and has become the very firstfruit of all that are dead." Verse 21, "For it was by a man, Adam, that death came and likewise by a man, Jesus Christ, that the resurrection of the dead has come."

Verse 22, "For just as through Adam ALL people that have ever lived die, likewise through Jesus ALL that have ever lived will be made alive, will be resurrected."

Verse 23, "But every man, woman and child shall be made alive in his own order (in series or succession), beginning with Jesus the firstfruit. Then, those that are the Messiah's chosen ones, the rest of the firstfruits, will be made alive at His coming.

Verse 24, "Looking forward to the completion of all His work of restoration, it will be then that Jesus will deliver the Government of God to His Father. This follows His having rendered inactive and inoperative all opposing rule, authority and power." (And, the rest of the dead will have been made alive in their own order.)

Verse 25, "Jesus must reign over the Kingdom of God until such time absolutely all of His enemies have been overcome."

Verse 26, "The last enemy to be rendered inactive and inoperative is death." (That is accomplished by making ALL alive.)

Verse 27, "God the Father will have accomplished His will and desire by successfully bringing ALL people to the point of voluntarily cooperating and accepting His Son Jesus. But when the Father says ALL are willingly submitting to Jesus, it is obvious that He is Himself excepted. For it is understood that it was He that brought ALL to that point of willing submission and acceptance of His Son."

Verse 28, "And when ALL people, ALL individuals, have come to voluntarily accept Jesus and receive His gift of salvation, then Jesus, the Son of God, will Himself willingly and voluntarily come under the authority of The Father. For it was He, The Father, who brought ALL people to accept Jesus and receive salvation. His plan, His will and His desire, will then be accomplished. ALL will have been brought to salvation. God will be totally and completely in all, He will be all in all."

# CHAPTER EIGHT

# REVIEW – REFLECT – REJOICE

I believe it will be helpful to take a few moments to review what has been presented in this book, to reflect upon it, and rejoice over the wonderful and glorious plan our great God is working out.

## REVIEW

In the last chapter, Chapter Seven, we looked at quite a number of scriptural passages which tell us of God's plan to bring ALL into His family. But, before any of us could grasp what has been inspired and presented in His Word, we needed to have many strongholds pulled down. (2 Cor. 10:4) The numerous teachings that we have been given, from childhood in most cases, prevent the many passages we looked at from even registering with us. Thayer's Greek Definitions defines "strongholds" as "anything on which one relies." Additionally he says, "of the arguments and reasonings by which a disputant endeavours to fortify his opinion and defend it against his opponent." The teaching we have received, be it true or not, places a terribly strong hold upon us. We looked at a number of common beliefs, that many of us have held, which argue against the passages we looked at in the last chapter. Let us review those briefly.

# FREE WILL

In Chapter One we looked to the Bible for revelation concerning God's will and the will of man. We looked at several passages of scripture which revealed that God is in absolute control, His will is supreme, and that will cannot be thwarted. Mankind's will, on the other hand, is naturally hostile and in enmity against God and anything concerning God. Man cannot and will not of his own will come to God seeking salvation. He has to be drawn or dragged. His will must be acted upon for it to be changed, for it to receive the faith of Jesus Christ and repentance that leads to salvation. God doesn't force men but will exert whatever is needed to bring about the change that is necessary.

When we look at the situation from a logical perspective, we can see that it is impossible for the Creator to make or create anything greater than Himself. He reveals Himself as the Master Potter, forming us, the vessels, as it pleases Him. God gave us freedom of choice, but He has also given us the instruction of what to choose. And, when it comes to salvation, He will do whatever is necessary to get us to change our will, our very nature. When He says that He wills all to be saved, His will won't be thwarted.

# Day of Salvation

We looked at the nearly universal belief of most Christians that now, today, before we die, we "must make our decision for Christ" or we will be eternally lost. In Chapter Two we looked at what the Bible reveals and saw it clearly spells out that not all will receive salvation at the same time. Some receive their salvation now, prior to Jesus' return. Others, alive when He returns, live into the 1000 years, often called the Millennium, and they and their offspring will be drawn, will be granted the faith and repentance needed, and will be given salvation. The vast majority, the small and the great, will be raised to life, each in his own order, during the Great White Throne period. They will be drawn, be given whatever is needed to assist them in changing the natural will, and will be reconciled to God and be given the gift of salvation.

# The Lake of Fire

Much has been preached and declared by numerous preachers and evangelists concerning the "lake of fire." We looked at the five verses in which the lake of fire is mentioned in Chapter Three. What we saw was a period of time in which those resurrected, the small and the great, would have the purifying work of God's Holy Spirit working to "burn out" the wood, hay, and stubble, the works of the flesh. The purifying will deal with the will of man, bringing each one to a revelation of their need for the Savior. Not force, but by revelation, they will be brought to SEE and KNOW God the Savior, and to see His love for them. When that all happens, they will receive the faith to be saved and will be given repentance. They will receive reconciliation and salvation.

## PREDESTINATION

One of the most debated of doctrines has been regarding the Bible's references to God having predestinated individuals to salvation. In Chapter Four we looked at this briefly. When we looked at the passages without the very strong holds of many of our previous teachings, it became clear. God, from before the foundation of the world, determined, predestinated, and declared that He "might gather in one all things in Christ." (Eph. 1:10) He didn't "predestinate" some to be saved and some to be lost. He is not a respecter of persons. He has determined ALL to be saved.

## THE UNPARDONABLE SIN

We devoted Chapter Five to a discussion of what many have come to label "the unpardonable sin." We looked at the context of the passages in Matthew 12 and Mark 3 where the religious leaders, the Pharisees, accused Jesus of casting out demons by the power of Beelzebub, "the prince of the devils." Jesus said to them that they were blaspheming the Holy Spirit. He tells them that "ALL manner of sin and blasphemy shall be forgiven unto men." (Matt. 12:31) But, He continues His remarks by telling them that the forgiveness for this sin would not be in the age He was addressing them in, nor would it be in the next age. The difficulty in understanding has been in the translation of the word *aion* from the Greek. The correct and easily understood translation would be "age" instead of "world."

None of us are in danger of a sin that can't be forgiven. Jesus told these individuals that even this grievous sin of blaspheming the Holy Spirit would be forgiven, just not until at least two ages had passed.

## UNIVERSALISM

It appears that almost all major Christian denominations and non-denominational churches believe that the concept of ALL mankind being saved is a false doctrine. And, as we covered in Chapter Six, many adherents to the concept believe that all will be saved no matter what they believe or what they do. There are others that do understand a bit more of what the Bible declares but still seem to lack much understanding. I didn't find a lot of detail in the stated beliefs of the Universalist Church, just the statement that "at last every individual of the human race shall become holy and happy." I feel we have presented more detail for you, the reader, to consider in the last chapter, Chapter Seven. I would encourage you to read through that chapter again, look up the referenced scriptures, and pray for revelation and understanding.

## REFLECT

There are a number of valid definitions of the word "reflect" but the one from Webster's dictionary that applies here is, "to think seriously, contemplate (on or upon)." Just quickly reading through the passages presented in Chapter Seven gives one a bit of a perception, but to really grasp and understand one needs to spend time seriously thinking about and meditating upon those scriptures. The key "ingredient" needed is God's Holy Spirit to lead us to the truth. I've already encouraged you, the reader, to re-read Chapter Seven. Take the time to meditate on and contemplate what is being presented to each of us. We'll briefly mention again a few of the powerful passages discussed for you to begin that contemplation and meditation.

## 1 TIMOTHY 2:3-4

The apostle Paul, writing to the evangelist Timothy, stated that it is good and acceptable "in the sight of God our Saviour; Who will have all men to be saved." Call to mind that we read that God is all powerful and that His "will" cannot be thwarted. Here, in this verse, it states that it is God "who will" have all men to be saved. The Greek word translated "will" here is *thelo*, and means "to will, have in mind, intend, to be resolved or determined, to purpose." Do we suppose that the One whose will can't be thwarted is unable to do what He intends, what He purposes to do? No, I should think not. If the all powerful God sets His will to do and accomplish something, He will do it! This is a positive and definite statement that ALL (meaning all, not just some) will be saved. Just think of that! Let your mind dwell on that for a bit. Imagine what this means. ALL, every man, woman, and child that has ever had life will be saved!

## 2 PETER 3:9

Peter tells us that the LORD is "not willing that any should perish, but that all should come to repentance." As we pointed out in our discussion of this verse in Chapter Seven, the word translated "willing" is the Greek word *boulomai*. It compares to the Greek word *thelo*. *Boulomai* is defined "to will deliberately, have a purpose, be minded." We are seeing once again that the will of God, that cannot be thwarted, is for none to perish. It is His will that all (the Greek word *pas* which means all, everyone) should come to repentance. We saw that faith for salvation comes from Jesus Christ and that repentance is also granted by Him. Both are given freely for each to receive salvation. It is God's will that ALL, each and every one, receive repentance, receive salvation. Once again, I appeal to each and every one of us, let us meditate, contemplate, and imagine what Peter is telling us here. ALL, every one, will be granted repentance, will come under the shed blood of Jesus Christ, have their sins forgiven, and will be given the gift of salvation! Let that sink in!

## 1 CORINTHIANS 15:20-28

The last passage we discussed in Chapter Seven was 1 Corinthians 15:20-28. We won't go through those verses here. I'll leave it to each of you, the readers, to go back and read those verses and the commentary. Meditate, contemplate, think about what the apostle Paul was telling us. He gives in those 9 verses an outline of God's plan for reconciliation and salvation of mankind. Most of us have read over theses verses numerous times without seeing and grasping what is there for us. Read, think about, meditate, contemplate the powerful and wonderful revelation contained there. Can we imagine and picture the end result that Paul tells us about? He states that after everything is accomplished by Jesus Christ, after all enemies are put under His feet, He turns everything back to the Father and "God may be all in all." Can we even begin to grasp what those words mean? ALL will be in the Father's family. ALL will be immortal sons of

God. ALL will be part of His plan, working, serving, praising Him for eternity!

# REJOICE

When I received the revelation of God's glorious plan for ALL of mankind I had to praise Him, thank Him, and rejoice! God has revealed Himself as LOVE. He doesn't just have love, He is love. We all have heard, and memorized, John 3:16, "For God so loved the world, that he gave his only begotten Son, that whosoever believeth in him should not perish, but have everlasting life." His love is for ALL the world's inhabitants, past, present, and future. As we read, God is no respecter of persons, His love is for ALL. We looked at the scriptures that tell us that He, in His great love, is unwilling that any should perish, that He wills all to be saved. For that we need to rejoice.

There are many reasons to rejoice. How wonderful it is to comprehend that the deep, heartfelt fears of so many people that their sons, daughters, or other loved ones would spend eternity in an ever burning, torturous, hell fire are unfounded. Hell, as commonly taught, is not based on the Bible. (That needs another book to explore.) God, a loving and perfect parent, is NOT going to put any of His children, whom He loved enough to send His son to die for, through such unimaginable pain, suffering, and torment. How we need to grasp this and rejoice!

We need to rejoice that we have a God who is LOVE, such love that NOTHING can separate us from it. Read with me Romans chapter 8, verses 38 and 39. "For I am persuaded, that neither death, nor life, nor angels, nor principalities, nor powers, nor things present, nor things to come, Nor height, nor depth, nor any creature, shall be able to separate us from the love of God, which is in Christ Jesus our LORD." It defies our imagination to think a God of such love would not have a wonderful plan whereby He brings ALL to reconciliation and salvation. Let us rejoice!

In the verses we just read we are told that there is absolutely NOTHING, ourselves included, that can separate us from God's love. His love is so great that NOTHING will prevent His plan of reconciling and saving each and every one. Some may try, resisting His drawing, BUT God's will cannot be thwarted! Let us rejoice in that! He is God who "worketh all things after the counsel of his own will." (Eph. 1:11) It is a "done deal"! As Paul told us, God "calleth those things which be not as though they were." (Rom. 4:17) We may not see it within the physical, BUT in the spiritual it is absolute. Praise God! Let us rejoice!

## FINAL COMMENTS

What has been presented in this short book is the greatest and most important revelation from God regarding what He has planned and is working out. It is the complete opposite of what most of us have been taught all of our lives. Many of you, the readers, are probably finding it hard to believe this could be true. Some, as I have personally seen, don't wish to believe it. For some reason they feel that it is somehow unfair to bring other sinners to repentance and reconciliation. Much like the workers in the vineyard, they believe that God is unfair if He gives ALL salvation. Let us get over such thinking. Can't we rejoice that God wants ALL in His family and has a glorious plan to make it happen?

# ABOUT THE AUTHOR

Garry D. Pifer has been a reader and student of the Bible for over sixty years. In the mid-nineties he embarked on a much more diligent study. He wrote most of his studies in article form, many being put onto the internet and some published in an independent journal. In 2020 he authored **God's Bestseller: Make It Real In Your Life!** This book is a handbook giving a step by step guide to studying the Bible, giving the reader the benefit of what he had learned over 25 years. Led by the Holy Spirit he has donated over 2400 copies to prisons and jails across America.

Garry and his wife, Connie, have been married for fifty-nine years. They are the parents of four grown children. They have eleven grandchildren and five great-grandchildren. They currently reside in South-Central Kentucky.

Garry may be contacted by writing to him at P. O. Box 131, Edmonton, KY 42129 or by E-mail: gdpifer@scrtc.com

# OTHER BOOKS BY GARRY D. PIFER

## GOD'S BESTSELLER: MAKE IT REAL IN YOUR LIFE!

Many have often wanted to understand the Bible but just thought it was a very confusing and closed book. In this conversational and straightforward book, Garry D. Pifer presents a step by step guide that will take you from a lack of understanding and a place of confusion to an opening up of what God has hidden FOR you, not from you. This book will give you direction in your search of the Scriptures. You will find priceless riches and treasures of great price. Read this book and learn how to find what has been concealed.

## SHADOWS OF JESUS IN THE EXODUS

Most have not grasped the numerous shadows in the Egyptian Passover and of the exodus of the Israelites from Egypt that have their fulfillment in the final days of Jesus, His death, burial, and resurrection. This study takes you through the many details of the exodus, establishing the timeline of the events, and moves on to the New Testament where the same timeline is revealed in the events of Jesus' final days and hours. Surprisingly you will find that many of the events did not occur on the days most Christians have been told that they happened. For an exciting study get and read **Shadows of Jesus in the Exodus**.

## THE HISTORY OF TITHING: WHERE ARE WE TODAY?

The doctrine of tithing 10% of one's income is taught in almost every church. Where and when did tithing begin, what was tithed upon, and to whom did it belong? Are we as new covenant believers under a command to tithe? For the complete history of tithing and whether it applies to you and me please obtain and read **The History of Tithing: Where Are We Today?**

## WHY AREN'T CHRISTIANS THE HEALTHIEST PEOPLE ON EARTH?

It seems that most Christians believe that God exists and that He is all powerful. Most believe that He is able to heal all sicknesses and diseases, but they are not sure that He will. Some believe that He brings sickness upon us to teach us lessons. Almost everyone appears to believe that God has given us the medical system for our health and healing and many aren't sure that divine healing is happening today. Why Aren't Christians the Healthiest People on Earth? looks at these beliefs and more. Garry D. Pifer will share his journey in the study of divine healing, looking at what the Bible reveals. What he discovered in his study may be totally contrary to what you have been taught and have believed from childhood. This challenging and thought provoking book can be read in one or two sittings but may lead to weeks and months of study and examination on your part.

## An Exposé of the Adversary

**An Exposé of the Adversary** looks at who the devil is, what his purpose is, where he came from, and the part he plays in our lives. **An Exposé of the Adversary** unveils and exposes the many lies he has foisted off on mankind, including the lie that Lucifer and Satan are his names. **An Exposé of the Adversary** dismantles his biggest lie, that he was an archangel that rebelled against God. Prepare to have the beliefs of a lifetime erased by **An Exposé of the Adversary.**

These books are available from Amazon and other major booksellers.

www.ingramcontent.com/pod-product-compliance
Lightning Source LLC
Chambersburg PA
CBHW060337130626
46553CB00003B/1035